OFF THE CLOCK

*An Unconventional Look at What Holds Us
Back at Work and What We Can Do About It*

C. P. MacMaster

Copyright © 2021 C. P. MacMaster

All rights reserved

Various names have been changed to respect the personal lives of the interviewees, but their words and voices have been faithfully respected.

No part of this book may be reproduced, or stored in a retrieval system, or transmitted in any form or by any means, electronic, mechanical, photocopying, recording, or otherwise, without express written permission of the publisher.

ISBN: 9798479516139
Imprint: Independently published

Cover design by: K.W.

For all those who still believe in the magic of their dreams; para mi Mami et Marie-Louise and Helen, Diane and Mara; for the finest magicians this believer has ever known, Carmen and Teo; for my beloved Pablo, you kept this book's path free of brambles and hecklers, and you held my heart even when it was too bitter for me to eat; and finally, for my father—Daddy, this was always, especially, for you.

PROLOGUE

The neighboring workstations felt as quiet as freshly loaded guns on a shooting range. I had to change something, anything. I downloaded a photo of a plump red blossom standing alone in a field, frozen in pixelated stasis on my desktop. I stared back, perversely satisfied. I was no longer frozen. I had just quit.

With only the thin whispers of a midcareer dream in hand, I had emptied the barrel of my loaded calendar. Shivering in the ensuing silence, I had just left a place we often fear, a place that locks us into dead-end jobs, miserable and underrecognized but too frightened or numb to see a way out.

My neophyte dream had started to speak up about a year or two before I quit while I thumbed page after page of business books and journals, my phone's backlight punctuating my insomnia. I loved my work, and I had great colleagues. But that wasn't enough. Why? I sought the kind of workplace stories that TED talks are made of, in hopes of dopamine-rich inspiration—something that might lubricate the old, rusty cogs in my mind. The stories fueled ideas, and the ideas were steering an off-the-clock conversation I wanted to have round-the-clock—stories and ideas I want to bring *here*, to you.

Having found the answer, at least for myself, I hope

to continue the dialogue with you by sharing these stories, statistics, and business theories to help you navigate your path to the professional fulfillment you are seeking. Your answer will be different, and maybe you'll find it quickly as you gaze outside your window to a vacant shop front or two years on when you speak before your team with your heart on your sleeve and their concentration suspended in the air before you.

There may be a (hopefully growing) portion of you who are happy in your jobs or who only relate to a few topics in this book; welcome! In the first half, I will address what makes us unhappy at work, and in the second half, I will talk about what we can do about it. Here's how these four major sections divvy up:

- **Section 1**: Starting with the (Wo)man in the Mirror: How Did I Get Here?
- **Section 2**: It's Not You: It's Them. Addressing the Hidden Obstacles at Work.
- **Section 3:** (Wo)man Up and Build Your Army.
- **Section 4:** Fish or Cut Bait! Deciding to Leave, Stay, Lead, or Pray.

Sections 1 and 2 explore what *we* do to make ourselves unhappy and how our work environments can (often unwittingly) block us. The second half of the book explores how to use the resources and relationships at hand to break through our workplace barriers. Section 4 concludes the book with an exploration of what your leap of faith might look like, with just a little more faith.

There is no question that more work can and must be done to make the labor market better for all. But what does that mean for me and you? The workplace frustrations I am going to address in this book are not one-dimensional problems but rather complex systems of individual and collective issues, with interlocking internal and external factors. At times it might feel overwhelming, and we might feel ill-equipped to change it. It would be easier to convince ourselves it is not that bad after all, but for how long can we continue pretending to quarantine the unhappiness we feel at work from the rest of our lives?

My answer is *not any longer,* and to realize any of our big hopes for a better workplace, we are going to need each other. Throughout my career, I have learned that I can't go anywhere without the trust, goodwill, and investment of my colleagues and professional network. The relational aspect of work is simply irreplaceable for delivering high-quality results. Just as off-the-record candor can make or break a business deal, the open conversations we are willing to have in our off-the-clock moments can reinforce the professional connections our career paths are built on. In the year after I broke the unspoken rule of quitting midcareer for little more than a pocketful of ideas, I have come to see those off-the-clock moments as precious. They made me realize that finding happiness at work not only made my work better, they were also crucial to my overall sense of belonging and well-being.

So, now, I will break another cardinal rule by spoiling the ending. It's simple: *connection*. Few evils survive in the face of it, and it is the inimitable foundation for building happiness at work or anywhere else in our lives. But what meaningful connection looks like for each of us is wildly different. So, let's get started!

SECTION 1: STARTING WITH THE (WO)MAN IN THE MIRROR: HOW DID I GET HERE?

CHAPTER ONE: HOW DID I GET HERE? MAKING YOUR NEXT CAREER MOVE

> *Without intending to, without even knowing it, he demonstrated with his life that his father had been right when he repeated until his dying day that there was no one with more common sense, no stonecutter more obstinate, no manager so lucid or dangerous, than a poet.*
>
> —GABRIEL GARCIA MARQUEZ, LOVE IN THE TIME OF CHOLERA[1]

It was a toilet. Just a toilet. Professor Standbright, in our lecture hall built like a Grecian theater, had projected a photo of Marcel Duchamp's Fountain signed "R. Mutt 1917." She asked whether art like this—arguably utilitarian—could be read as a commentary on the banality of production, commerce, and society, and were these creative elements enough in their totality for protection under copyright laws? I was perplexed and, for the first time in years of university, completely hooked. It was a moment of validation; maybe I had made the right choice for a career path even if it had not been wholly expected.

Then again, studying law is probably one of those safe choices that most parents would sanction heartily. One Former First Lady of the United States would likely agree. Like many of us, Michelle Robinson had grown up doing what she felt was expected of her. She had studied piano with her grandmother and applied herself in school. One of the very few Black students to be accepted to Princeton, Robinson graduated cum laude and went on to study law at Harvard. She landed a snazzy law firm job back home in Chicago. She was doing everything right, but she could not shake the feeling that she had more to offer. Her beloved father had recently passed away, heightening her sense that time was nothing to waste. She contacted every lawyer she knew who had left the practice of law. One meeting led to another and then to a scribbled note for the hiring manager to interview the woman behind the impressive résumé. Then the deputy chief of staff at the Chicago mayor's office, Valerie Jarrett, remembers the subsequent interview[2] with the twenty-six-year-old, who possessed a confidence and composure Jarrett had rarely seen in one so young. An hour later, Jarrett offered Robinson the job, to which Robinson replied she would need to think about it.

Robinson was preparing to make the first real swerve of her life, inspired and supported by her exceptionally talented fiancé, Barack Obama, a man who had already made a name for himself by becoming the first Black president of the century-old *Harvard Law Journal*. After requesting the unusual step of introducing Jarrett to her fiancé over dinner, Robinson took the job and never looked back. Her (and her future husband's) commitment to public service took her down a path to becoming the first Black

First Lady. She believes there is no one way to a successful career, "Now I think it's one of the most useless questions an adult can ask a child—'What do you want to be when you grow up?' As if growing up is finite. As if at some point you become something and that's the end.[3]"

Some of you will have picked up this book because you are unhappy with your job, your boss, and your team, and you want out. Perhaps you took the job because you needed the money or someone pushed you to, and somewhere along the line you stopped trying for the career of your dreams. If I were to ask, "Are you happy with your career?" you might bitingly reply, "What career?" Our first order of business is to consider how we get into the careers (or jobs) we have.

Career choice expert Dr. John D. Krumboltz recounts a question he liked to pose to career counselors attending his workshops: "'You are now employed as a career counselor. Had you decided to become a career counselor when you were 18 years old?' So far, the number of career counselors answering yes is zero."[4] He was trying to illustrate, with a bit of dry humor, that sheer aspiration cannot be the sole or even strongest factor relevant for understanding career choice when so many of our childhood dreams differ from the jobs we do today.

Krumboltz's happenstance learning theory suggests that many factors influence career outcomes, such as genetics, realizations arising from the analysis of self and others, caretaker and peer attachments, and education. Moreover, Krumboltz also considered the effects of an "imperfect world" that include many other societal factors that prejudice or advantage people and groups of people. Identifying and separating the factors that are static from those that are malleable is crucial in deciding what is the right career move.[5]

What we cannot change we can accept and then move on; what we can change requires and deserves our attention and energy.

Early on in his work, Krumboltz[6] identified the destructive power of some of those malleable factors, specifically such defeatist internal refrains as:

- "If I can't have the best, I don't want anything at all."
- "If I don't make more money than my father [or mother], I'll consider myself a failure in life."
- "If I fail, I feel better knowing that I had not tried very hard."
- "If I only could do this, then I would be happy."

These refrains can have as much power over our careers as our education and societal opportunities by creating false narratives that handicap, for example, our willingness to try new things, speak up, or invest in relationships. Like mental cockroaches, they persist and reproduce, blackening the terrain of our will and drive. That is why it is important to cultivate a thick skin and seek out the honest opinions of our formal or informal counselors, colleagues, and friends. Their tough love can help you see these refrains for what they are and fumigate relentlessly.

Unsurprisingly, Krumboltz regards the belief that people simply grow into their careers as a societal fallacy. He looks to various internal and external factors, behaviors, and conditions as to why people pursue the careers they have. The questions we ask ourselves, our external influences, and our internal reactions to them very much shape the course of our careers, whether we see them for what they are or not. Nevertheless, he does not dismiss the power of individual agency. Understanding our motivations to take a transformative step in our work life can be as crucial as the step itself. To a statement like "I don't have a career," he might say that simply because we cannot trace our career choice to (a) singular, or discrete, event(s) does not mean we should not be intentional now about what we seek and the options available to us. In other words, whether or not we think we have a career does not take us off the hook for being intentional about our professions today.

Being intentional about your profession might mean moving to another job. Most workers in the United States today will change their jobs several times. Career coach Ashley Stahl states that three out of four Americans have changed their careers at least once and that as many as one out of three are considering it at any given time.[7] According to research from LinkedIn,[8] the average number of employees who have changed jobs in the first five years after graduation has nearly doubled in the last twenty years. For the average thirty-two-year-old in 2016, that meant having already had four different employers.[9] Job-hopping in general has been increasing since the 1990s, though some also pin the trend on the Great Recession (2007–2009), which pushed scores of people into new jobs and loosened the ties of loyalty between employer and employee.

Like many mid-thirty-year-olds, Joanne[10] has held four different jobs in the last handful of years. Each move has been essentially a promotion or a better opportunity. I asked her what she felt had influenced her career and what she had expected to do growing up. In grade school, she had excelled in sports and math. Wanting to keep her options open, she studied international business, finance, and languages in college. Passionate about different cultures, foods, and outdoor sports, she moved her consultancy business to the French countryside. After a few years, she realized she missed office comradery and looked for an office job. One job followed another as she got promotions and better jobs. In some ways as predictable as a Gantt chart, Joanne would nonetheless balk at the notion that her career has been the result of one thing, or even one dream. Recognizing the multiple factors in her background that have shaped her career, she chalks up much of her success to taking a risk on opportunities that offered her a chance to problem-solve complex issues involving global partners and stakeholders—something she really cares about and is motivated by. Instead of blindly chasing some two-dimensional image of a perfect job, she has followed her principles and passions to jobs that felt right for her, and it has been the secret of her success.

Bill, a lawyer who like most attorneys had a career trajectory that had been largely driven by the first few jobs he landed, let me in on another secret early on during my university days. In his experience, few attorneys knew at graduation what they would specialize in. He had become a small-town general practitioner with a bent toward real estate because of his early mentors and experiences.

The fantasy that great thinkers and leader are preternaturally called to their vocations is seductive, but the truth is that as we continue along our careers, we make choices. These choices add up like lumpy piles of clothing. We have worn them in success and in failure, leaving behind a closet of possible past selves we can no longer fit into. But in that time, we have built a style, a persona. Once we can face that, we can move on to decide what we want and who we are for the "now" and the "next."

Shopping for a new job, position, or career can be a daunting endeavor, but there are steps that we can take to make it more manageable. Like many career coaches, Stahl[11] suggests four steps, in addition to using reliable career assessment tools, to finding the right job:

- List your options.
- Look for person-to-organization synergy.

- Network. Network. Network!
- Call on your mentor(s).

A tried-but-true approach to figuring out your next career move is to list your options and the factors that are relevant to your choice. American polymath and forefather Benjamin Franklin wrote[12] that in making a decision he would dutifully list the pros and cons, each of equal weight, and scratch them off by pairs until he found a tie-tipping reason. Whether it is done talking to a friend or literally penning a list, identifying options ultimately helps narrow down the choices. A new dad or mom considering whether to go part-time might weigh such factors as possible career aspirations, workload, and effective salary. The new parent will also weigh his or her preferences for child-rearing and quality of life. That being said, lists of options or answers are only as good as their questions—so the utility of this process is inextricably tied to your willingness to be honest with yourself. For many, returning to the office is a welcome respite. For some, the opposite is painfully true. Neither is right or wrong; they are merely factors we must consider.

Looking for an organizational match is another powerful component of your decisional framework, particularly for professionals who have been in their field for a few years. Comparing your skillset and strengths with what companies need and what is currently being untapped requires (1) self-awareness; (2) knowledge of the market and current trends; and, quite frankly, (3) chutzpah. Corporate leaders might recognize the intersection of those three factors as also being the sweet spot for founding a new company, striking out in a new direction, or building a great team. Practically speaking, it means your homework is not done after you have studied a prospective employer. You should match your list of strengths (coupled with examples you could provide in an interview) to their current and future needs before you can hope to convince them of the sagacity of employing you.

For executive positions, an understanding of this three-part framework is a prerequisite; however, applicants who can present this synthesis clearly and compellingly will stand out every single time.

Networking is also key to leveraging potential for the right career move. As much as 85% of candidates land a gig through their connections. [13] Especially in small job markets, networking can make the difference between landing a coveted job and lingering on the few open candidate lists. Samta is a scientist, policy advocate, and fierce mother of school-age kids. When I asked her what had made the biggest difference in her career, her reply was short and sweet: *"Why, my network, of course!"*

Samta proceeded to illustrate her belief in the power of good networking with a story about how she had landed her penultimate job. She had been one of thousands of candidates for an international post in public health and had feared her application would be lost in the morass. She decided to make a few calls to mentors and colleagues from different countries who were connected to the post in hopes that they could create a buzz for her candidature. It worked. She was called into the interview by a panel that had been directed to the selling points of her profile, and she landed the job. Moreover, the job opportunity could not have come at a better time. Samta had just moved from her natal town in Southeast Asia back to the city where she had previously landed a sizeable research grant and delivered stunning career-defining results.

I asked Samta how she had navigated the abrupt return, and she replied that she had activated her network before she arrived home. She contacted her ever-patient doctoral advisor and a former supervisor to let them know she was looking for a job. Leveraging the success at her previous role, she was able to find an attractive national public health position quickly. She owed it to the networking of her former boss and thesis adviser, who had bent many an ear in the process of helping place her. Did she consider them mentors, I asked? Why, yes, she revered them as mentors and as role models. They were women who believed in and supported other women. They had not only guided her academic and professional work; they had seen Samta—the woman—and nurtured her ambition and hefty intellect.

A similarly named executive coach once hammered me over the head with the refrain *tout est réseau*. Everyone can be included in your network; when you are looking to make a move, consider every classmate, teacher, colleague, friend, fellow parent, neighbor, business partner, vendor, club member, and acquaintance as the person who could get you that one pivotal step closer to the right job. Having helped hundreds if not thousands find c-suite positions in a tight job market, this executive coach has seen the wisdom of her words confirmed time and again.

With the ubiquity of social media and mobile phones, remaining connected is, practically speaking, as easy as hitting a button. Reaching out to our network for help to get a job, however, remains daunting. American singer Amanda Palmer recalls the power of humbling herself and learning the "art of asking" while working as a street performer for the five years after her graduation from a well-regarded liberal arts college and touring with her eclectic indie band."[14] Calling the five years of street performance as an eight-foot statue, dressed in a white wedding dress and standing on a produce crate, the best training she could have had for her burgeoning music career, Palmer practiced vulnerability in a visceral, at times painful, way. Drivers would yell at her to get a job, while lonely passersby connected with her in silent and intense exchange as if to say, "Thank you, I see you," and "No one ever sees me, thank you."

Leaving her music label after a so-called failure selling twenty-five thousand album copies in the first weeks, Palmer took the lessons from the street to her music career and convinced her band to give away their music for free, instead merely asking their fans for financial support in an unprecedented music-based crowdfunding project. She reached 1.2 million USD in donations. It was a bewildering success. Many criticized her techniques, calling it begging or degrading, implying weakness in the asking for help. To the contrary, it is the very vulnerability of the ask that is so powerful—the faith in the fairness of exchange, however it may manifest. Palmer believes that people, fundamentally, want to help. When it comes to finding a job, it is the vulnerability in the ask that calls to our helpful natures.

The vulnerability practiced by successful askers requires a strong sense of self in addition to a thick skin and a healthy attention to our motivations. For many of us, that includes recognizing the confounding aspects of our desire to please, especially for professional women. Often, we chase perfection and hide behind a self-effacing sense of service.

Growing up a chubby and sensitive Latina in a middle-class Anglo-American neighborhood, I had felt continually on the margin of social interactions, locked outside a virtual greenhouse of life where friendship, community, and belongingness flourished. A raging introvert, I spent my childhood in my own thoughts. Medicine seemed like a safe bet, so I declared a major in psychology during my university's summer orientation, with the expectation that I would become a psychiatrist. What better study could there be for me, therefore, than that of the mind itself?

I picked up classes that awakened a sense of identity and community in me: Latin American Masculinity and Gender, Caribbean Women Writers, Women's Poetry and Latina Feminist Literature. I read Latina and Black-American powerhouses like bell hooks, Sandra Cisneros, Maya Angelou, Isabelle Allende, Toni Morrison, and Gloria E. Anzaldúa, writers who explored themes of gender, sexuality, child-rearing, socioeconomics, race, and politics. I had turned a corner and imagined I would go toward a career in academia to study intersectionality, sexuality, community, and identity. But the shift from literature and cultural studies toward law would prove as abrupt as my shift away from psychiatry to literature.

I was driving my faithful Jeep when my mother, sitting next to me and listening to my intentions of pursuing a doctorate in Women's Studies, exhorted, *"Pero, si tu eres una mujer!"* It was not the response I expected. Of course, I was a woman, but Women's Studies was not about studying my own performance of womanhood (well, at least not directly). I tried to convince my *Mami* of the lofty nature of my aspirations. I reiterated my professor's question on our first day of class: "What is a woman?" She had challenged every simplistic definition, social, genetic, or otherwise, that my classmates could offer and had thrown me into a silent tumult debating central cases and exceptions, sociocultural constructs, autonomous ideation.

My mom, too, fell silent, and I gripped the steering wheel as we swiftly rolled across a strip of Florida highway that was like a flat swath of leather drying under a scorching sky. Breaking through my obstinate silence and changing the course of my life, my mother posed a simple question: *"¿Y qué pasó con tu sueño de ser abogada?"*

My answer to that set off a series of events that ultimately led me to accepting a job offer 4,600 miles away four years later, on a continent where I had never stepped foot, a mere ten days after taking the bar exam. Oddly, I was not afraid. I had been reticent to move a handful of states north, but somehow the offer of moving to Europe filled my belly with a calming sense of direction. Far from the intractable certainty at the beginning of movies, it was the kind of low-call gut-feeling that is easy to miss but indispensable in making the right move.

I started this chapter with a quote from Colombian writer Gabriel Garcia Marquez's *Love in the Time of Cholera*. You probably wondered what the common sense, obstinance, lucidity, and danger of poets has to do with your career; for the curmudgeonly among you, perhaps nothing. As flagbearers of transformation, however, exceptional poems can be as disruptive as their authors.

A sonnet can melt a beloved into a babbling pool of reverie while a satire can expose delusions and doublespeak, setting off the forces needed to topple corrupt systems. There can be a madness in poets and disruptors. The same mad whisper can also pop up over furtive coffees and games of *what would you do if you couldn't be an office administrator or a marketing specialist or a team manager*. There is a kind of madness required to live a life worth dying for and, correspondingly, to cultivate a career worth living for. There is a kind of bravery required to honestly see your job prospects. And, perhaps, a poet's obstinance is required to activate the connections in your life and a poet's lucidity is required to lace up the shoes on your intuition while facing the unknown dangers that sublimate life-changing sprints.

Moreover, the love and sweat artists put into their creations transform not only the "nothing" to the "something"—the porcelain urinal to the iconic piece of art—but the work itself also transforms the artist.

Careers do the same, for better or for worse. After quitting my job, my appreciation for the passage of time deepened, like it had for Michelle Obama when she realized she needed to leave the practice of law for public service or when Samta knew it was time to change continents for her family. Therefore, let us not waste time stalling the search of our life's fulfillment but rather consider the totality of the personal, social, and professional factors that drive and affect us in this—as Krumboltz would call it—"imperfect world" and take the first step.

The next step is to leverage your passions and your network to the task of finding a job in an organization to which your skills and experiences match. Like Joanne moving her consultancy work so she could relocate to the French countryside or Samta engaging with her network to ensure she landed on her feet as she moved from one continent to another and back, you can more easily exploit unexpected or unorthodox opportunities if you know what drives you instead of chasing a static image of perfection. As media mogul and philanthropist Oprah Winfrey said in her Harvard University commencement address:

No matter what challenges or setbacks or disappointments you may encounter along the way, you will find true success and happiness if you have only one goal, there really is only one, and that is this: to fulfill the highest most truthful expression of yourself as a human being.[15]

But what if you have not felt like yourself in a few years?

CHAPTER TWO: THIS IS NOT YOUR DAD'S MIDLIFE CRISIS

Midway along the journey of our life
I woke to find myself in a dark wood,
for I had wandered off from the straight path.
How hard it is to tell what it was like,
this wood of wilderness, savage and stubborn
(the thought of it brings back all my old fears),
a bitter place! Death could scarce be bitterer.

—DANTE ALIGHIERI, THE DIVINE COMEDY [16]

Just a few months over forty, Miguel sat in front of me, pushing his carrots and peas around the plate. Clean-shaven with a medium build, he tends to blend into a crowd. We were sitting in a 1970s-style cafeteria with yellow tables and hanging ferns. After a deep sigh, he looked up and said,

It's like this: All my life, I've been running towards what I wanted. I got good grades. I got the degree. I got the girl and the kids and the house and car. We finished all the remodeling. I've been here eleven years including the break when we went

> abroad. We've had hundreds of BBQs, drank barrels of French wine and ate crates of swiss cheese. My daughter is trilingual. But it never feels like enough. I should be happy, but I don't feel it.

Many of us have felt like Miguel. Many of life's big, shaping decisions are past us: what to study, how to make money, who we want in or consider as our immediate family; and yet our satisfaction tanks feel empty, unjustifiably siphoned away when they should have been full. With no obvious culprit to blame, we wonder if our lives would have been better had we studied something else, worked somewhere else, or married someone else. Outwardly, we say we are lucky, but we secretly worry that the "reward" will be merely more of the same. Is this as good as it gets? As certain birthdays loom around the corner, we start to wonder, "Could I be having a midlife crisis? But I'm too [young, old, successful, happily married...]!" The poster child of a toupee'd fifty-year-old man driving his hot new wife in a red car has been replaced by the circuit-training forty-year-old with a monthly subscription for imported coffee. In short, the midlife crisis has had its own midlife crisis.

Over half a century ago, Canadian psychologist Elliott Jaques coined the term *midlife crisis* when he published in 1965 an article in the *International Journal of Psychoanalysis* entitled "Death and the Midlife Crisis."[17] Writing at a time when global life expectancy was about fifty-five years (almost two decades less than today),[18] Jaques envisaged midlife crisis as a phenomenon typically occurring between the mid-to-late thirties and presumed it was related to declining sexuality and fertility.[19] He examined a handful of artists' lives and concluded that midlife was a time when artists either came into their power or saw it die away.

For examples of those who came into their power at midlife, Jaques pointed to artists like Paul Gaugin, who gave up his banker's career at thirty-three to become an established painter by thirty-nine, Donatello's style change at thirty-nine from controlled statuesque balance to lush and immediate expression or Goethe's coming into his genius between thirty-seven and thirty-nine through a marked evolution in his writing.

In Jaques' view, other artists burned out after midlife. According to Jaques, Francisco Goya's most-acclaimed paintings appeared before forty, as did Ben Jonson's best plays, before forty-three. Michelangelo lived in relative artistic silence for fifteen years after he finished the Sistine Chapel and *Moses* before producing the Medici monument and *The Last Judgment*. Jaques also considered deaths during midlife as support for this hypothesis, noting the deaths of Wolfgang Amadeus Mozart at thirty-five, the Italian painter Raphael at thirty-seven, Polish composer and pianist Frédéric Chopin at thirty-nine, and French poet Charles Baudelaire at forty-six.

Jaques' argued that early-blooming artists enjoyed (or suffered) feverish eruptions of fully formed creation, whereas older artists tended to feed cooler, more deliberate furnaces. For the latter, Jaques looked at Sigmund Freud as an example. Freud produced his preliminary theories of psychoanalysis in his thirties and was widely using the term *psychoanalysis* by his forties. According to Jaques' interview with one of Freud's acquaintances, Freud had once advised, "Write it, write it, put it down in black and white…get it out, produce it, make something of it—outside you, that is; give it an existence independently of you."

Some of you will balk at Jaques' suggestion that midlife is a product of sexual decline or his cherry-picked analysis of (male) artists' lives as either starting or stopping in midlife, and I would not disagree with you. But I wonder if there is potential for using his construct to test a hypothesis at the proverbial watercooler that simultaneously permits both inclusive application and a nuanced space for the highs and lows of midlife. I'll cut to the chase:

What if we looked at midlife as a second adolescence between adulthood and our final years?

Kieran Setiya was only thirty-five years old when he felt a vice of "nostalgia, regret, claustrophobia, emptiness, and fear" squeezing his mind as he looked down the path of his life. The road signs ahead warned NO PASSING ZONE while he did the same job day in and day out for a few more decades until the exit for "retirement," which would unwind inevitably into deterioration and demise. Setiya was a philosophy professor at the University of Pittsburgh when he was having what he recognized as a midlife crisis.[20] True to his trade, he turned to philosophy and history, noting in his book on his midlife crisis, *Midlife: A Philosophical Guide*, that "until around the eighteenth century, there was no sharp line between moral philosophy and self-help."[21]

According to Setiya, French historian Philippe Ariès (known for identifying childhood as a social construct in the 1960s) had traced back the "feeling of personal failure at midlife to the experience of the 'rich, powerful or learned man of the late Middle Ages' who had luxuries of aspirations denied to the inhabitants of traditional societies."[22] While recognizing the danger of speculating about the mental history of writers and artists long since deceased, Setiya held out Italian writer Dante Alighieri, who was banished from Florence in 1302 at age thirty-seven, as an example of such a man. It is tempting to see Dante's *The Divine Comedy*, where the narrator passes through hell, purgatory, and paradise after being lost in a dark wood sometime "midway along the journey of life,"[23] as suggestive of Dante's own midlife crisis.

However, this is not likely the first written reference to a midlife crisis. Setiya states that the earliest text he found as precedent for midlife crisis was written almost four thousand years ago in Egypt and contained a conversation between a man and his soul, although it was unclear to Setiya whether the weariness was a result of a sense of critical personal inadequacy or merely the man's particular circumstances.[24] Nevertheless, the tension between the common (Is this just another one of life's phases?) and the personal (Is it me or my choices?) seems to be an inescapable facet of midlife crisis, just as it was for my friend, Miguel.

During my lunch with Miguel, I had asked him if he considered giving his reflections, in Freud's words, "an existence independent of himself"? Could he at least identify what gave him the highest sense of fulfillment or happiness in his life? His response was immediate: "Pushing myself, pushing boundaries, physically and mentally," he said. He gave me an example from his professional and personal life. He felt satisfaction in the moment before a large, pricey project finally landed approval. It was in the struggle during small competitions at his circuit-training club. It was in the hot press of urgency and danger when something great was only around the corner of exertion and desire, but once captured, that something great was never quite great enough.

What made the inexplicable emptiness worse was that Miguel was also shouldering the guilt of his inability to feel sustained joy, like the dead weight of an albatross he himself had shot.[25] He might push himself at weightlifting or spend hours crafting a compelling employee value proposition for the many businesses that consulted him, but as the win faded, he had to keep chasing the fleeting moments of cathartic joy.

He tried practicing gratitude after we talked about a TED Talk[26] from David Steindl-Rast, a Catholic monk and interfaith scholar. Steindl-Rast argues that true happiness does not come from money or health or safety or status. These things can make life more comfortable, of course, but real lasting happiness springs from gratitude. Steindl-Rast takes the example of people who have suffered great atrocities and yet could find joy in their gratitude for surviving, or for what was not taken from them, or for the renewed possibility of each day.

Miguel searched for small moments to be grateful for on a daily basis, to the exclusion of generalities like a "good life" or a "good job." He already knew that when he tried to appreciate the totality of the good things in his life his next thought was on what seemed missing or incomplete. Moreover, summoning physical elation over his good life was about as easy as remaining aware of his socked toes. Simply put, he was used to it and figured breaking down that "good life" into smaller chunks of perceptible enjoyment was more digestible.

"I get it. It's like the difference between money in the bank or in your hand. A hundred bucks in the bank might not feel like much. But a crisp hundred in your hand? That's real," I interjected.

I had come across the practice of gratitude shortly after a pivotal career move. I had sought advice from Kimberly, a stylish powerhouse of a corporate professional based in London. With superficial incongruity, she also happened to be a certified minister. Having known me since I was a fresh-faced twenty-year-old, Kimberly has been a singular and cherished mentor, so I jumped at the chance to have dinner with her when she was passing through.

Like many young professionals, I was having trouble getting accustomed to old school mentalities about the impossibility of change or improvement that can sometimes litter a workplace. I wondered how long I could keep my optimism up. Kimberly listened as I gave examples of poorly reasoned arguments and defensive stances. What could I do? Tell the boss? Talk to HR? Hit the resignation button? Ever the wise diplomat and earnest listener, Kimberly quietly searched my face as I spoke and then said, "You will find your answers on your path towards gratitude."

As I told the story to Miguel, I joked that had Kimberly and I not been indulging in a piping hot fondue and a large, chilled bottle of white wine, I would have thought I was sitting before a famished monk offering a cryptic homily.

Kimberly had pressed on, saying she believed that God lights our paths in moments of simple gratitude. She had mentioned books and online talks that guided my gratitude exercises, often during my walk to work. Nothing was too small or simple, like "I am grateful for this tree with its elegant and heavy branches full of pale-yellow leaves," or "I am grateful the kids did not fight this morning, and they even put on their rainboots without complaining."

On most days I probably forget, but I find the practice entering my weekly thoughts and conversations. Like any practice, it becomes not only easier and more automatic, but the capacity for joy from these small moments of gratitude becomes amplified. The practice of gratitude makes me more likely to stop to praise my children for a job well done, or to voice my appreciation of the beautiful park that flanks their school, or to admire a meal delectably well executed. Like pearls, these moments string up into long luminous ribbons of contentment and peace, or at least they had for me. I asked Miguel if he had enjoyed the exercises.

"*Pues, si.* Each day I wrote down the thing I was grateful for… the moments I had to play with Luz, just the two of us, beating my record for time, polishing off Fran at CrossFit last Tuesday… Stuff like that."

"So how do you feel?" I asked.

"The same. I was happy for those moments, but yeah, I feel the same, generally," he replied.

Frustrated that I did not have more to offer my friend, I turned to another mentor, Robert. A no-nonsense diplomat, Robert was not surprised by Miguel's reaction. "Gratitude is not enough. An exercise like that would not work for me. If you're unhappy, do something. Move, find another job, get out of a bad relationship," he said. Robert was somebody who thrived in high-stress, high-stakes situations and had met personal and professional success by deliberately and decisively moving around the chess pieces in his life. It had not been a changed perspective but rather changed circumstances that had led him out of the ebbs of his life.

It turns out that neither Miguel nor Robert is alone in his experience of midlife crisis. By the 1990s, the study of midlife crisis as such had itself reached forty. At the John D. and Catherine T. MacArthur Foundation Research Network on Successful Midlife Development (MIDMAC), researchers questioned whether midlife was a universally difficult period.[27] It was one of the first times a serious study had been given to the question of well-being of people between the ages of thirty and seventy. The MIDMAC research analyzed eleven different studies canvassing about eight thousand American men and women between the ages of twenty-five and seventy-four (in addition to comparative studies in England, Germany, and India to control for cultural differences). In the main survey, identical questions were sent out, with 750 of the responders being additionally assigned to small groups for follow-up qualitative research.

The main survey came out with a surprising result: Most people in the huge tranche of middle age actually felt quite calm, enjoyed stable relationships, experienced relative job security, and had good health. Additionally, the older the participant was at the time of the study, the later they defined "midlife." Men and women between twenty-five and thirty-four imagined forty and forty-three, respectively, to be the start of midlife, whereas men and women from sixty-four to seventy-four said that midlife started at forty-six and forty-nine, respectively. Regardless of age, however, the participants agreed that midlife lasted about fifteen years.

In the small groups, just under a quarter had experienced a midlife crisis, most of whom attributed their crisis to traumatic factors beyond their age. With the research results showing that only one out of four might experience a midlife crisis, Elliot Jaques' notion that midlife crisis itself is an inevitable phenomenon of aging, declining sexuality, or a change of creative energies had been turned on its head.

A decade later, conceptions of midlife would continue to evolve while advancements in medicine, technology, and global living conditions drove rates of life expectancy from the mid-fifties to a record-breaking seventy years.[28] A 2008 study headed by David G. Blanchflower and Andrew J. Oswald from Dartmouth University questioned whether the variations of well-being over a lifetime were actually more like a U-shape, meaning that feelings of well-being were high in youth, dipped in midlife, and climbed back up in later years.[29]

The concept of midlife as a commonly difficult period was back in play. But did most people experience midlife as a crisis, or was it just a dip in happiness?

Before weighing in on that question, the researchers noted an important caveat. A variable dependent on age could be confounded by an uncontrolled cohort factor; in other words, certain generations might have had it better or worse (and at different times), thereby skewing their individual perception of happiness. That being said, the researchers did confirm their conclusions across seventy-two countries,[30] from Argentina, Australia, and Azerbaijan to Uruguay, the United States, and Uzbekistan, giving at least some comfort against the cohort effect, since global events generally affect certain regions more than others. To that point, the lowest point for well-being was not the same country to country.

For an American male, 52.9 years marked the minimum-happiness age after controlling for income, education, and marital status, as opposed to European men, who hit their lowest point of satisfaction quite a bit sooner at 44.5 years old. Noting that European women and men were in step, unlike American females who reported their well-being "rock bottom" at 38.6 years of age, it will be interesting to see if the American difference will level out between genders over time.[31]

Even accounting for subtleties like the cohort effect, the prospect that midlife might be a dip in well-being for almost everyone felt somehow comforting (as in "this too shall pass"), and I was almost ready to share my reading with Miguel.

Curious to hear another perspective, I called up my oldest friend in Geneva for coffee. In his mid-thirties, Andy has lived in more than half a dozen countries across Europe and Africa, speaks seven languages, and is married to a beautiful Big Four analyst from his home country of Albania. I figured if anyone could understand what Miguel was going through, it was Andy. He did. With his legs crossed but his arms open in a pose simultaneously reluctant and forthcoming, Andy ruminated silently before saying, "I just wonder if I fit, in this time and this place." Explaining that our phones were constantly buzzing, and picking up his own phone to prove it, he added, "At every corner we are being marketed to, our attention being forcefully grabbed, and our inner peace being disturbed."

There was always something. Always moving, we hurry to work, rush through our grocery shopping, sprint to pick up the kids, lumber through dinner before collapsing in front of a TV flashing perfectly criminal, perfectly shabby, or perfectly polished lives in between jarring sales pitches. Deeply in love with his wife and toddler, Andy fought hard for the life he enjoys, although, like so many of us, he finds it increasingly difficult to enjoy pockets of quiet simplicity, the kind that inundated his student days before he entered the complex web of responsibility in his thirties.

Is yearning for the pleasures of youth merely an inevitable consequence of midlife? Almost imperceptibly, in our thirties and forties, we inevitably become the bastions of *home* and *work* as we pick up the mantle of society from our parents and grandparents. We are infiltrating the ranks of management and entrepreneurship. We are building new families as our parents prepare for retirement. We have tasted enough of life to understand that some choices are permanent while still feeling we could change our lives completely with the signing of a new employment contract or resignation letter, marriage contract, or purchase deed, secondary education application, or request for a first round of IVF. It is a recipe for an existential crisis.

My conversations with Miguel seemed like the tip of an iceberg. The more I asked, the more I heard, "Maybe I *am* having a midlife crisis." Another friend, Laura, called me up shortly after my chat with Andy. She wanted to catch up over burgers and cheeky beers. When we met at our favorite spot near the local university, she said business was good but, as was typical for a freelancer, quite unpredictable. She had managed to make a living for herself for three years, but she was not sure for how much longer she would want to jump from assignment to assignment. I figured she at least had the stability of her home and her girlfriend. "Oh, we've broken up, and I'm moving out. I'm not sure where I might relocate. You might say I'm having a proper midlife crisis," she said half-laughing and half-pleading. Like me, Laura is stuck squarely in the middle of two generational behemoths: millennials and Generation Xers, and I suspect as millennials age, social media will become inundated with chatter about midlife crisis.

Many women born between 1965 and 1984 (Generation X) may feel that the current dialogue about midlife crisis remains skewed toward the *Miguels* instead of the *Manuelas*, so to speak.[32] This "latchkey generation," growing up after a baby bust as mothers increasingly joined the workforce and childcare options were few, is often characterized as cynical, disaffected, and, even now, highly stressed out.[33] Members of this generation are unnerved by the balding sports car driver, the corporate-suit-cum-beet-farmer, and the circuit-training Daddy[34]—tropes that have become entrenched in our collective psyche as an acceptable "exit lane" for men. Where are the models of midlife (crisis or not) for women?

Moreover, Gen Xers are likely to keep an unfulfilling job only for the money. Having grown up during the recession of the 1990s, followed by a jobless recovery, then hitting the early 2000s dot.com bust and, of course, the Great Recession of 2008, many find themselves exhausted from having bare-knuckled it crisis after crisis.

Convinced that midlife crisis was neither a monolith nor a myth after talking with successful-but-dissatisfied Miguel, action-driven Robert, modernity-skeptic Andy, and life-reformist Laura, I felt better educated but still yearned for a magic bullet. Online searches offered up a fifteen-point Q&A featuring advice like: *If you are confused and lacking direction, take a step back, find where you lost the path, and make a plan to get back on it*,[35] or a ten-point guide warning against impulse purchases and rash breakups.[36] Do nothing, or do something, or change your mindset; it all felt the same.

I bumped into Miguel at a Colombian party celebrating the pregnancy of one of our mutual friends. He came alone. I asked about his usual entourage, and he said his wife's parents had the kids back in Spain for the weekend while she was away on a "girls' trip, or whatever." He turned as he spoke, almost waving away the thought of her, and I began to worry that a breakup might be imminent. Maybe his crisis would finally crack on the altar of divorce.

Months turned into a year, but he did not break up. He did not quit his job or pitch up for a PhD on the intersection of enology and gender. Instead, he dove into his work—

letting himself get energized by his team, continuing his circuit training, playing with his kids, focusing on reconnecting with his partner, and booking a babysitter as often as he could. He leaned on a close group of male friends living through some of the same problems, even if their own paths had become drastically different to his. "Yeah, I'm good. Things are good," he said casually as we toasted at a birthday party recently. I marveled at how well he appeared.

The magic bullet had been time—that all-healing salve—and maybe, if I dare say, connection to others who were going through the same thing.

Whether midlife can be a crisis of declining sexuality and volatile shifts in creativity as psychologist Elliot Jaques originally hypothesized, a journey of existential questioning as it was for history professor Kieran Setiya, a period of relative calm like the MacArthur Foundation researchers saw it in the 1990s, or the dip in U-shaped perception of well-being over a lifetime as the Dartmouth analysts concluded in the early 2000s, midlife is ultimately an individual experience, colored by the circumstances of our lives and desires. If the promising tunnel toward professional success seems to have ended in a fool's gold mine, it can feel like a bad case of buyer's remorse.

The solutions are the same: Return it, keep it, or make something out of it.

CHAPTER THREE: REFOCUSING THE LENS AFTER DISAPPOINTMENT

> *My grandmother had a very interesting theory; she said that each of us is born with a box of matches inside us but we can't strike them all by ourselves [...]. Each person has to discover what will set off those explosions in order to live, since the combustion that occurs when one of them is ignited is what nourishes the soul [...]. If one doesn't find out in time what will set off these explosions, the box of matches dampens, and not a single match will ever be lit.*
>
> —LAURA ESQUIVEL, LIKE WATER FOR CHOCOLATE[37]

Chosen Last: Being Passed Over for a Professional Opportunity

When Mariluz's contract was the sole contract not to be renewed in her sizeable team at a small start-up, her boss called her into his office to apologize, saying it was out of his hands. "He said I had the intelligence, the work ethic, the results, but not the demeanor. Or at least that is what he said his boss had said," Mariluz explained. Listening to the explanations in stunned silence, I heard Mariluz utter what she felt was her fatal mistake: failing to keep her place.

We were sitting on a clean, well-worn wooden bench in a small dog walking park behind her new workplace near the United Nations headquarters. Incredulous, I asked if that was all she got by way of justification.

"That was it. After years of 'excellent' work, these were the best excuses I was offered. But I was told that my wanting to have a baby was also brought up," said Mariluz. My mouth dropped. "Apparently they debated the issue, *mi'ja*," said Mariluz.

Now well into her career at a human rights organization, Mariluz considered her story a cautionary tale, for Latinas in particular. Stories of your personal life should never reach the ears of your superiors as this might give them "ammunition." She said to be careful of sharing too many of your ideas, too. A supervisor who feels imminently more comfortable with men will be quick to prefer your ideas when male colleagues utter them, so don't share any part of your thought process with some dude at the office! Mariluz further cautioned, "And don't ever let them see you sweat."

We finished our sandwiches, looking out on the parking lot–sized garden that was glowing in the early afternoon light like a crisp emerald. Mariluz put away her designer sunglasses —the only hint of personality in her uniform of a white shell, black pants, and black flats. She could have sold vacuums or religious texts door to door. She was curating her looks as ruthlessly as she cultivated her pessimism. What had been the cost of her forcing down the hot pain of her first professional disappointment, particularly one that had attacked her as a person? To simply remove any outward appearance of that person. Carmen Miranda had become Gumby, devoid of flare, charisma, and authenticity. She had been passed over for the job opportunity, but she could not make peace with *why*. Mariluz is not alone. Sixty-one percent of three-thousand people who responded to a 2017 Monster.com survey reported having been passed over for a promotion or award in the workplace.[38]

The first thing to do is to get the facts but tread carefully. Deborah Brown-Volkman, a career coach from New York, recommends a discussion with your manager only after emotions have settled. Managers may be reticent to give honest feedback when it comes to passing someone over. She suggests explicitly asking for honest feedback, even if it may hurt, by granting the manager "permission to speak freely."

Searching for a manager's perspective, I asked my no-nonsense mentor and friend Robert what he thought of the advice. "Regardless of how good someone is, there is always competition," said Robert, who has managed teams of all sizes in the United States and across Europe. Robert continued:

> *I welcome the opportunity to give back specific feedback. I would be open to explaining that someone else ticked more of the boxes that we needed. They might then ask, 'Which boxes did I miss?' And, fair enough, I would go through it with them.*

> *We could discuss their experience, or anything missing from the interview process, etc.*

Robert admits that it would be quite different if the colleague were visibly upset. At that point, he might invite them to return after more reflection to increase the effectiveness of the conversation. Other factors such as seniority or place along the application process would weigh on the amount of detail Robert would recommend giving. If someone was not suitable for the position to start off, then Robert would take it as an important lesson learned that he failed to properly screen the candidate at the outset and then would take more time than would be usual to let him or her down easily.

For Mariluz, her supervisor's biggest fear seemed to be that she would reproach him and question why he did not extend her a new contract despite her stellar performance record and appreciated intellect. Mariluz, sure of herself and the integrity of her work, did not confront him and instead chose to go about her business with her head held high and her nose to the grindstone. The price, however, was clearly weighing on her, even years later as we sat having our brown bag lunch on a park bench. I wondered whether she might have learned a great deal had she decided to confront him openly and professionally (even if it had only been to seek future employment with an emphasis on diversity and inclusion.) To do so, she would have had to have opened the discussion with an appreciation of his time and a request that he speak to her freely and frankly. What would have come after would have been out of her hands, but in fearing disappointment, she all but secured it.

So I asked Robert what he would recommend to someone who could not shake the lingering feeling of disappointment after a conversation at the workplace about being passed over for a new opportunity. He replied simply, "If you can't answer the question 'Where do I want to be and what do I want to do?' stay where you are. Devote the energy to figuring it out, but sometimes you just have to ride it out. There is nothing more you can do. But isn't that life?"

If you are facing a similar situation, regardless of your conclusion on next steps (We will get to more of that in section 4: Fish or Cut Bait! Deciding to Leave, Stay, Lead, or Pray), the bravest thing right now is to stop, take a hard look at what happened, and try to make sense of it as best you can with the information you have. Maybe there is something you will change about yourself, your job, or your environment. Perhaps the change needs to be external, or both internal and external. Either way, consider whether you can learn from this situation. If you can, you have not lost.

Impostor Syndrome: Passing Yourself Over

For others, the question is not one of landing the dream job—you have already got it. Your performance is stellar, and you are widely respected. But you are racked with the fear of being found wanting. Secretly, you do not think you are enough and see constant flaws with your work. You feel like an impostor or fraud waiting to be found out. If this does not apply to your personal situation, feel free to skip ahead to the last bit of this chapter concerning burnout. Or skip ahead to the second section, It's Not You: It's Them. Addressing the Hidden Obstacles at Work.

The first to study and name the "impostor phenomenon" (also called impostorism, impostor syndrome, and the impostor experience) were Dr. Pauline Rose Clance and Dr. Suzanne Imes, who published their findings in 1978.[39]

They studied 150 high-achieving women over five years, many with advanced degrees and respected reputations from various fields, as well as high-achieving students. The majority of the women were White university students between twenty and forty-five years old. Regardless of the honors degrees, praise, and recognition these women received, many of them felt like they did not deserve their success. They felt like "impostors." Some felt they had gotten into their respective programs by mistake.

Believing at the time that the syndrome only affected women, the researchers were quick to conclude that, "thus, unlike men, who tend to own success as attributable to a quality inherent in themselves, women are more likely either to project the cause of success outward to an external cause (luck) or to a temporary internal quality (effort) that they do not equate with inherent ability."[40] Drs. Clance and Imes further asserted that the "phenomenon may be further maintained in response to the negative consequences that are likely to befall the woman in our society who displays confidence in her ability."[41] In 1985, Dr. Clance published her book *The Impostor Phenomenon: Overcoming the Fear that Haunts Your Success*[42] but did not conclude until 1993 that men too experienced impostor syndrome.[43] The researcher also made a startling discovery: Self-esteem was not connected to impostor syndrome, accounting "for only 9% of the variance in impostor phenomenon scores."[44] However, anxiety and introversion did seem to go hand in hand with impostor syndrome.

Dr. Clance also reviewed research that correlated impostor syndrome with the belief that intelligence was a fixed entity rather than a malleable trait, such that inadequacy was a direct result of limited intelligence. They also found indications that sufferers of impostor syndrome often came from family backgrounds where a significant emphasis was placed on appearances, communal cohesion, and rules. Overall, impostor syndrome taps into the fear of failure, the inclination to attribute any success to luck or temporary effort, and the desire to stand out coupled with a need to consistently downplay recognition from others, the fear of evaluation and that success cannot be repeated, and a belief of being less capable than one's peers.

Matilde grew up as the daughter upon whom all East-meets-West parental expectations weighed. She was shepherded into advanced programs from an early age. She traveled, picking up degrees from renowned European universities, and shot up the ranks in a small cash-poor nonprofit. Not yet forty, she was made director of a brand-new program aimed at helping young women. Her expectations for herself are high, but she never meets them. She wonders if she chose the right vocation or has done enough to leave real lasting impact. She cringes at every coaching opportunity that forces her to talk about herself and sit through analyses of her personality, strengths, and failings. She is also the first person who ever spoke to me about impostor syndrome.

"Oh yeah, I constantly think whether what I am doing is not enough, and whether people will see it for what it is," she said to me before sipping her coffee. My eyebrows shot up. "Really? But I thought you were doing well. You just got that promotion," I replied. She picked up a biscotti with her ringed fingers, lifted a corner of her mouth, glanced quickly to the side, shrugged. I searched her face for clues about the reason for these feelings and to better understand what she meant. Was her nonchalance a mask?

Not necessarily. Since Dr. Clance's research shows that

while self-esteem is not positively correlated with impostor syndrome, a person exhibiting impostor syndrome may have a sense of self-esteem that "is precarious, requiring a system of defenses that is taxing and anxiety-producing. Impostors are motivated to [look smart]. Impostors' worries about their impression on others indicates a high vulnerability to feelings of shame and unworthiness."[45]

Changing the internal dialogue with roleplaying can help. By "playing" the part of a colleague, teacher, or loved one who has offered positive feedback in the past, either in individual or group therapy, you can experience a sense of feeling worthy and appreciated for your success. Another good idea that Matilde tried out to success is to keep records of positive feedback, to help you be more objective when it comes to your performance. Just plain old talking with others can also help. If one person is willing to share her feelings, others might feel more comfortable to share as well. Ultimately, the hope is that in realizing we are not alone, we can turn the internal dialogue around.

Even when we do not suffer from impostor syndrome, we can face strong (unfounded) feelings of inadequacy in the workplace. Far from feeling like an impostor, Sébastien, a store manager of a bustling luxury goods store, bemoans the tendency of the French educational system to engrain a certain pessimism and overreliance on hierarchy and power systems. As a young professional, he rose through the ranks of retail in a region where managerial styles often overemphasized following procedure, doing as one is told, and highlighting faults over praising successes. Always pushing himself, he nevertheless kept striving for more and found himself led to a company with an American work culture.

Inspired by a new sense of independence and encouraged

by positive feedback, Sébastien threw himself and his team into new challenges without the expectation of throwing their failures in their face, but with the hope that in moving them out of their comfort zone and showing them real trust, they would be inspired and would grow. A fervent believer of striving for excellence and a good old-fashioned people person, he boosted his store's customer service rating within a few months and landed his team an award for the most improved client experience in Europe. Indefatigable, he continued to improve, leading his team to win the award for a second year in a row, along with one recognizing sales performance.

He has started to let himself enjoy the fruits of his own successes, but he still finds it hard to accept a compliment. During a beautifully appointed meal, I asked Sébastien whether he believed that owning success could be a birthplace for strength and vulnerability. A knowing smile shot to his face. He agreed. It is so much harder to believe we deserve recognition for our hard work, knowing better than anyone the faults within it and ourselves. But to accept responsibility for that which we struggle with and to still want more is where the real growth lies.

I discussed the issue with a close confident, Didi, by comparing coaching a team with raising children. When they are angry with themselves for doing something naughty and getting caught, they might claim they are never good. They are bad kids, they will say. Do not let them; instead, say they are not allowed to play the victims of their imagined inadequacies. They are good kids who sometimes make mistakes. Didi nodded vigorously in reply, adding that for children of immigrants, as we both are, the lectures of inadequacy and keeping our heads down are only that much more complex in modern workplaces where vestiges of colonialism persist.

We all make mistakes and hiding behind a feigned "Oh, but I am only this or I'm only that" only triggers our victimhood and blocks us from growing, Didi said. We can be good and still make mistakes; the challenge is to learn from them. Others will numb their emotional circuitry in hopes that failure will be less of a shock. It is a strategy that works only far too well, as it also numbs joy when victory does come around. The strength in being vulnerable is in taking it all—the good and the bad—and still standing in the arena, as Dr. Brené Brown author of *Daring Greatly*,[46] says.

Sébastien is not the only one who has struggled to acknowledge his own power, authenticity, and vulnerability. Working for a large recruiting agency, Gloria is a twenty-something professional with a winning smile and a secret. She moved to Geneva as a teenager, the daughter of French expats who moved from Europe to the United States and then back again. Proving the veracity of Didi's words, Gloria feels the pull of not meeting expectations, especially those she sets for herself. We met for lunch and talked about impostor syndrome. After I introduced the concept, she instantly proclaimed, "But that's me! As soon as I feel I am about to get evaluated or I've been praised for my professionalism, I think if they knew me, maybe it wouldn't really be enough."

Changing our inner monologue is no easy feat, but it is essential. Even the most confident among us can feel the cold slimy hand of insecurity on our backs. Formal therapy, roleplaying, and talking it out with a sympathetic partner or friend can go a long way to helping to change the false narratives we often cling to. Regardless of whether the disappointment was triggered by failing to get the job, like Mariluz, or struggling to face the fear of failure and learning to truly feel success, like Matilde, Sébastien, or Gloria, satisfying career growth hinges on taking a healthy dose of fearlessness and perspective to support self-discovery. It is work worth doing.

Ready to Pass Out: Addressing Burnout

But what if that work feels undoable? For some, disappointment, frustration, and stress can turn into burnout. German-American psychologist Herbert Freudenberger coined the term burnout in 1974, [47] after he noticed that the veins of long-term drug addicts would "burn out" from abusing narcotics injections and started using the term for staff exhaustion. Soon after, psychologist Christina Maslach and Susan E. Jackson picked it up and ran with it, developing the Maslach Burnout Inventory.[48] The version of the inventory that is used for most occupations focuses on three essential factors:
  - physical and emotional exhaustion,
  - cynicism about work,
  - and the feeling of lost professional efficacy.[49]

Definitions of burnout vary from country to country,[50] but they generally center around the notion of emotional and physical collapse from overwork. Surprisingly, the United States does not include burnout in the Diagnostic and Statistical Manual of Mental Disorders, Fifth Edition.[51] In Europe, the highest rates of workplace burnout occur in Turkey, Albania, Serbia, and France.[52] According to an Utrecht University study from 2018, about 10% of the European workforce feels burned out, compared to 17% of other countries. Within Europe, rates varied from 4.3% in Finland to 20.6% in Slovenia, in comparison to other non-EU countries, ranging from 13% in Albania to 25% in Turkey.

Burnout has been recognized as a serious challenge to the bottom-line, including for founders and entrepreneurs who may push themselves past physical and emotional limits to a fault.[53] Rates of burnout pose a problem for larger companies as well. In a 2013 Gallup Report, only 13% of employees worldwide reporting feeling proactively engaged and committed to the growth and development of their employer. Disengaged employees outnumbered these motivated few by two-to-one. Gallup's data suggested that the 70% of the American workforce who did not identify as being proactively engaged cost companies up to 550 billion USD every year because of their increased absenteeism, likelihood of stealing, and poor treatment of customers.[54]

According to a research survey of employees of the University of Zaragoza entitled "Coping with Stress and Types of Burnout: Explanatory Power of Different Coping Strategies,"[55] there are three types of burnout:
- the "frenetic" burnout type that features exhaustion from incessantly working toward success past the point of overload and saturation;
- the "under-challenged" burnout type—otherwise known as "bore-out," which features such monotony and underuse as to bring apathy and disengagement; and
- the "worn-out" type that develops in the absence of appreciation and gratification to the point of neglect and a feeling of loss of control.

I had never heard of the bore-out type until I met Katarina. Her company had been bought by another, and her position was going to become obsolete. She was given a leave package that allowed her almost half a year of transition. She started looking for another job immediately, but her tasks were drastically reduced. She was suddenly facing hours upon hours to accomplish a task that took her minutes. An adamant professional, she sought out work as much as she could. She took longer lunches and tried to fill her workdays with productive tasks that would keep her motivated.

Within a few months, Katarina started to succumb to depression and feelings of inadequacy. She saw her doctor, and he immediately put her on leave. She needed respite from the daily reminder that she was being ousted and had still not found a job that suited. At home, she slept a lot and leaned on her affectionate partner. She started working out more and doing small things to take care of herself. Luckily, Katarina found a job in a dynamic and challenging environment. When I saw her again, she looked at least five or seven years younger. For her, time off from work, exercise, and personal connection were the cures.

No one is immune to burnout, including the young and healthy. By some reports, millennials (born roughly between 1980 and 2000[56]) are particularly sensitive to it.[57] According to a 2018 Gallup study of about 7,500 full-time American employees, 28% of millennials reported feeling frequently or constantly burned out at work compared to 21% of their older colleagues. Almost 70% of millennials surveyed reported feeling burnout at least at one point in their work lives.

The cures for burnout include physical exercise, engaging in real (not virtual) personal connection, time off from work, and individual or group therapy, in addition to more work-based approaches like seeking more motivating work and working with others on stimulating projects.[58] American attorney Paula Davis-Laack felt the crippling weight of burnout while she was practicing commercial real estate law before she found herself on medical leave. Deciding to leave the law, returning to school to study psychology and later opening the Davis Laack Stress & Resilience Institute, she says that for organizations wishing to avoid as well as address burnout, leadership is key. "Good leadership in healthcare organizations, whether in the form of an inspiring manager, getting regular feedback, or simply knowing that your leader has your back, can help prevent burnout."[59]

Disappointment at work can come in many forms: rejection for a new job or contract extension, suffering silently with impostor syndrome, or feeling the crushing blow of burnout. The first half of the battle is facing the situation for what it is—calling it out, by its name, and then sharing the name and seeking guidance and support.

Some of that work may involve developing and adopting different coping strategies or seeking honest feedback, but it may also include looking at a situation for what it is. If you are like me, it is easier to blame yourself for your situation. You can change yourself but not others or your company. But sometimes, the fault is in our surroundings, and no one amount of self-work can substitute for seeing your workplace situation for what it is.

SECTION 2: IT'S NOT YOU: IT'S THEM. ADDRESSING THE HIDDEN OBSTACLES AT WORK.

CHAPTER FOUR: TOXIC WORK CULTURE - IT TAKES JUST ONE ROTTEN APPLE TO SPOIL THE BARREL

> *Words are things. You must be careful, careful about calling people out of their names, using racial pejoratives and sexual pejoratives and all that ignorance. Don't do that. Someday we'll be able to measure the power of words. I think they are things. They get on the walls. They get in your wallpaper. They get in your rugs, in your upholstery, and your clothes, and finally into you.*
>
> —DR. MAYA ANGELOU[60]

The daily drip of venom from the lips of a toxic colleague can collect inside us, slowly shutting down our creativity, energy, and productivity. As Dr. Angelou said, words get into you. Likewise, since words have power, calling out a toxic relationship at the office can help create a shield against it, help us disengage from the polarizing person, and help us avoid reinforcing their negative behavior with attention. You can avoid letting them get a rise out of you or taking their negativity personally.

Toxic relationships negatively impact our health and well-being. Even when factoring out gender, age, marital status, ethnicity, body mass index, employment level, smoking, physical activity, nutrition, and common mental disorders, those of us with negative close relationships are 10% chubbier.[61]

The reasons why include many things. Having negative feelings about someone at work can "increase physiological arousal either through activation of the hypothalamic–pituitary–adrenal axis or through the fight-or-flight response and the secretion of adrenal medullary hormones."[62] Then we feel the need to blow off steam, which drives us to a cinnamon roll with our midmorning coffee or to the local pub for an after-work pint and basket of hand-cut chips. This, in turn, decreases the chances that stress relief will be managed through physical exercise. Finally, it can end up negatively affecting our heart health (literally, not just metaphorically).

A common way for toxic relationships to start is through regular contact with the "Coworker from Hell—just about every company has one...more if you're particularly unfortunate. They come in all shapes and sizes. The Diva. The Know-It-All. The Complainer. The Suck Up. The Bully. The Back-Stabber."[63] Each is different, and each of these types is nonetheless a toxic influence at the office. Divas suck the energy out of the room, wasting time bringing the attention back to themselves with an inflated sense of importance. Regardless of their actual authority, they will rule with an iron fist, keeping information to themselves and pitting others against each other. Divas can easily create Complainers and Suck Ups around them, who often hide their incompetence and lack of creativity behind diatribes and dissent. Always silent when it comes time to suggest ideas, Complainers thrive by criticizing ideas and predicting failure, guaranteeing the latter by offering no help or constructive contributions. Suck Ups, in turn, gravitate around Divas and authority figures, grasping at the trail of someone else's star. Just like Complainers, they are equally unyoked by responsibility and often blame someone else for their failures.

The Bully and the Back-Stabber are some of the hardest to deal with since they actively aggress their colleagues. The difference of course is whether they do it on the surface or behind the scenes. Bullies often hide their insecurities behind passive-aggressive or direct attacks, insults, and mockery of their colleagues, whereas Back-Stabbers concentrate their energy on destroying reputations and relationships by sowing mistrust and rumors through the gossip mill.

One of the most pernicious is the Jekyll-and-Hyde type, who pretends to be your friend outside the office to gain your trust and then takes advantage of your relationships, standing, ideas, or energy at work. Colleagues like this might be liberal with boozy dinner invitations until they get caught taking notes during a wine-fueled binge, later passing off other's theories and proposals as their own. They are excellent gaslighters, who delight in making their colleagues doubt their instincts and discredit themselves in front of others. Since unmasking these kinds of toxic colleagues can be tricky, a checklist can help:[64]

> "When you're with the person, do you usually feel content, even energized? Or do you often feel unfulfilled and drained?

After you spend time with him or her, do you usually feel better or worse about yourself? Do you feel physically and or emotionally safe with this person, or do you ever feel threatened or in danger? Is there an equal 'give and take,' or do you feel like you're always giving, and he or she is always taking? Is the relationship characterized by feelings of security and contentment, or drama and angst? Do you feel like he or she is happy with who you are, or do you feel like you have to change to make him or her happy?"

You might notice warning signs: treating the administrative or support staff badly, speaking poorly of officemates or even family members, speaking with envy of others' visible projects, a hot temper, and a general lack of patience. Particularly with first-time jobs, it is easy to cling to early office relationships in an unhealthy way without seeing their effect on performance or perception. As many will attest, what is said is one thing and what is written is another. In other words, no amount of promises, handshakes, or good intentions should ever make you silence the rumble in your gut that says, *Don't trust them.*

Sometimes the rotten apple is not a person or group of persons but a work culture that results in company-wide demoralization. Ineffective, aggressive, apathetic, or disingenuous leadership is a powerful source of demoralization in a company, no matter what the size. Simon Sinek's TED Talk[65] and book *Why Leaders Eat Last: Why Some Teams Pull Together and Others Don't*[66] look at the power of positive, service-oriented leadership and the importance of safety in the workplace. In it, he talks about the biochemical reasons we are built to seek and sustain positive kinships in the family and our community. The key to this connection is called *oxytocin*.

Oxytocin is a powerful hormone, accountable for the elated feeling we get when we are falling in love, eating chocolate, or meeting up with a new friend. It is a critical biological element of our relationships that encourages us to make the social connections needed for the execution of our social contracts[67]—the commitments that make us part of a broader community, bolster leadership, and ensure survival.[68] Analyzing the corporate world as a composite of mammalian herds, Sinek posits that leaders are given their place as "alpha" by the tribe with the expectation that they in turn protect and guide their tribe.[69] In exchange, alphas get a place of respect with accompanying privileges and decision-making powers. The whole exchange is awash with feel-good oxytocin responses. Coupled with our unique ability to believe in ideas and form coalitions around them,[70] bonding, particularly in complex multiperson groupings, is how we humans have survived over tens of thousands of years. The problem comes when our leaders keep that coveted spot of alpha, with all the benefits of status, without protecting their tribe(s).

Simon Sinek paints a picture of gazelles on the savanna.[71] Without knowing what the danger is, if one gazelle startles at the fear of an upcoming danger, the fear transfers through the herd with a ripple effect. We are the same. At the mention of cuts or a new boss, fear runs through a corporate community as it runs through a startled herd of gazelles. The team becomes saturated with the cortisol, the hormone in charge of our flight or fight response.[72] With cortisol constantly dripping into our veins, we cannot sustain growth, which erodes the meaningful bonds at work. No longer a team, employees become self-interested and trapped in a cycle of anxiety and diminished productivity that failed leaders have themselves to blame for.

To turn a toxic (demotivated) team around, leaders have to give their employees facetime and patience. Emails and money are a poor substitute. Biochemically, we require that hit of oxytocin we get when we are forming and nurturing relationships with our leaders and watching them do well by others as well.[73] The funny thing about oxytocin is that we get a bump of it not only when we are forming relationships (as in the classic example of when mothers are flushed with oxytocin while giving birth so as to ensure and promote early bonding) but when we do good for another, receive help, or even just witness it.[74]

Toxic behaviors can creep up slowly, often from the best of intentions. Augustine is a new manager who wants his team to feel supported. He asks where they are on all their projects during never-ending roundtable team meetings. He sends them a book that inspired him, but he limits his office hours. He hears from other managers that some in his team are underperforming. So, he decides to take on a tough-love attitude when they present their ideas, asking, "Why?" and "How do you know?" so often that he gets lost in the role of Socratic investigator and fails to note their emotional withdrawal. On Augustine's team, not everyone is a star or in the stage of their life when they can exert maximum effort without detriment to their personal relationships. High potentials feel micromanaged and frustrated. The quiet ones, some with impressive former titles or hidden genius, withdraw into their protective shells, sticking their necks out only when the coast is clear. Many people stop voicing their opinions, or at least their real opinions, out of fear for a tongue-lashing.

Augustine continues to climb the corporate ladder, further exposed and stressed, constantly bucking under the scrutiny but desperate for the affirmative reinforcement of his superiors. When upper management pulls him in contradictory directions —innovate but do not fail, excel in new ways but do not take any risk—he leans on his team's talent. He has created a self-fulfilling prophecy with those he expects to underperform, granting facetime and validation to the others. He says he believes in his team and would defend them against anyone, except, of course, *himself*.

It is tempting to blame Augustine's problems on him, but middle management is often reflective of the failure of senior management to support and protect *them*, as some of you managers out there will recognize. For example, when middle managers are blamed out-of-hand by senior management for their underlings' failures (perceived or actual) without explanation or allowance for innovation and its twin sister, failure, middle management can end up with a no-win situation. Their teams become listless and stifled. The team can feel oppressed by the need to always justify and explain every action, decision, and plan. The manager feels overwhelmed by the responsibility for a team that begins to underperform and the pressure imposed by senior management that gives no room for failure, experimentation, or support.

Management is not alone, of course. Human Resources (HR) can be a strategic partner in cultivating and maintaining a positive work culture that should not be ignored. Unfortunately, the role of HR is frequently downplayed or disregarded when things are going well,[75] causing companies to miss the importance of work culture until they are trapped in a toxic flight or fight cycle. At that point, HR (a victim, perpetrator, or knowing abettor of that same toxic culture) will scarcely have the bandwidth to help its company without an external buoy.

A long-time consultant and author advising on organizational change, Tricia Emerson states[76] that work "culture is deeply entrenched, and changing it is like shifting the course of a river. If we want to truly change the river of culture, we need dynamite and dams—drastic measures reserved for an organization in existential crisis." This means starting with quick incisions into the organization to remove toxic colleagues, regardless of performance, and old symbols of the previous culture, including office routines, physical office setup, hierarchy and salary bands, meeting methods, and even brand names. A key aspect here, however, is the communication regarding the moves and the desired end-goal.

Emerson advocates for a critical mass of people in the change management, including senior managers, HR, and communication teams, and this critical mass needs to be truly on board. Another essential factor is to move quickly, e.g., within ninety days while tracking the progress across a published action plan, including possibly those terminations I mentioned. It is exceptionally critical to communicate clearly and neutrally to those guilty of maintaining the toxic work culture by giving situation-based feedback and concrete timelines with consequences before using the last resort of termination. Employing ambiguity or generalities in an effort to avoid hurt feelings or outrage can leave staff abandoned in the cortisol-rich aftermath of unexpected and unexplained layoffs.

In the words of a CEO of an international nonprofit organization in Geneva, Frederick, terminations even among curmudgeonly senior officers can do more harm than good when executed poorly. Having worked in a fast-paced private sector job before arriving to shake things up in a gentlemanly-paced NGO, Frederick believes first and foremost in people and their capacity. I joined him for coffee at his office, which features a humble but sturdy wooden table flanked by black leather chairs. Recognizing that people can become bastions of the toxic old guard, he believes every opportunity should be given to warn senior management of the envisaged changes in concrete terms. He acknowledges that turning a toxic work culture around is a delicate task that balances the repercussions of termination with the likelihood of rehabilitation and the impact of inertia.

After cracking the fossilized underbelly of a toxic culture, the next steps involve establishing the desired work culture. This means doing more than printing out an employee brand proposition, handing out shirts at a staff event, singing kumbaya, and crossing your fingers. The real question is: What does that work culture look like for the company? What behaviors are best suited to replace the behaviors from the past? A difficult aspect of this process is, of course, having the courage to name and own the unacceptable behaviors. Colleagues, especially senior leaders, who were not cut away in the first incision but still participated in the toxicity would have to own their past behaviors and enunciate as well as model the required new behaviors. That means that senior leaders and executives need to understand and be aligned with the message. Emerson recommends establishing a clear outline for change using the following framework, answering each of these questions with one word:

- What problem are you trying to solve?
- What is the solution to it?
- What approach are you using to implement that solution?
- What do you expect the result to be?

Finally, all the changes must be sustainable. Infrastructure should be built around training, monitoring, and celebrating progress to ensure that the positive change that cost so much effort to instill is not lost. That being said, without support from top management, organizational change of this nature is simply impossible.

According to one American study, as many as one out of ten companies have a toxic work culture.[77] A powerful example is Microsoft.[78] When the new Microsoft CEO[79] Satya Nadella started in 2014, he required all his executives to read *Nonviolent Communication* by psychologist Marshall B. Rosenberg. Microsoft had become a shattered workplace where teams competed with each other with hostility and disloyalty. The tenets of nonviolent communication that Nadella wanted to instill were the following. First, look and understand. Pay attention to the behavior you are witnessing. Describe it neutrally. Second, explain how you feel about what you are seeing, and then connect your feelings to the behavior that you are witnessing. Finally, address what you want by requesting the concrete remedial actions.

An example of this kind of communication might be:

You presented my three-year compliance policy and practices without recognizing my role or inviting me to participate. I feel undervalued, manipulated, and desperately frustrated. This lack of recognition, and the missed opportunity to present my work to the board of directors for one of my most significant projects, gives me great concern for my career development. The next time there is an opportunity for me to present my work to our superiors I request your support and encouragement, to help me grow and learn.

Another key aspect of what the new Microsoft CEO implemented was to break down silos and reorganize the corporate structure to blast away the vestiges of old team rivalries. The rise and fall of Microsoft before that time had been dramatic.[80] Bill Gates and Paul Allen came together in the early 1970s to create an operating program for a new, faster computer. A couple of years later, the company dubbed Microsoft took off as personal computers became more and more popular and licensing money kept rolling in. Soon Gates and Allen were looking for someone with more managerial and business experience. They turned to their friend from Harvard, Steve Ballmer, who had worked briefly at Proctor & Gamble. He had the tough guy demeanor they felt could lead the business side of things. Shortly thereafter, in 1992, Bill Gates was named the richest man in the world by *Forbes*, and then Windows came out with its graphic interface featuring a desktop and icons in 1995. The company had reached its zenith of cool. The Empire State Building was gussied up in the Windows colors: yellow, green, and red—incredibly, for a product launch.

By the 1997, more than 85% of all personal computers in the United States were running Windows. The program was the behemoth success that Microsoft could not think around. Engineers had come up with a prototype e-book, but since Windows was a clunky operating system for such a device, Gates iced it. The group that had dreamed up the prototype e-reader got removed from a direct reporting line to Gates and was dumped under the group in charge of Microsoft Office. The time for trial and error was over. Inevitably, the product was pushed to market too soon, missing key features like light, small screens and easy-to-read digital "pages" that the later generation of e-readers would succeed at providing. Moreover, the original design was supposed to run with touch screen technology that would later become popular with Apple's iPhone. Microsoft had been the first to seed but left before the harvest.

On December 30, 1999, Microsoft's stock started to fall and almost two weeks later, Bill Gates would turn over the reins as CEO to Steve Ballmer. Employees hired after the millionaire-making days would work alongside their elder colleagues, creating unspoken rifts and slights. Then came a performance review system called "stack ranking" that would force managers to grade their team on a forced bell curve, regardless of actual performance.

Quickly, people realized that the way to more money was through turf wars so they wasted energy besting rivals instead of bettering their offerings. Just as they had missed the e-readers, Microsoft would miss the smartphone revolution, despite having developed an operating system that could be used for pocket devices.

For Microsoft, it would not be until a new CEO was named in 2014 that the culture would be challenged. The culture fix seems to be paying off. Annual revenue crossed 100 billion USD in the fiscal year ending in June of 2018 (the highest in its forty-three-year history), driven by demand for the company's cloud computing business products. And Microsoft's stock price has tripled since Nadella took charge. The stellar share price and financial performance speak to his success, say analysts, in changing investors' perceptions of Microsoft as outdated and declining.[81]

Ultimately, the importance of having a productive work culture is more than just being humane or seeking a comfortable nine-to-five job. It means more money at the end of the day. It might even be the first interview question you ask when offered the traditional interviewer's prompt, "Do you have any questions for me?" You can change a salary or a title but changing the work culture is an exceptionally complex endeavor that must come from the top; you want to be very careful considering the work culture in evaluating any potential workplace.

CHAPTER FIVE: A SMILING FACE HIDES A HISSING SNARL - RACIAL BIAS AND DISCRIMINATION TODAY

> *Can you explain to me how Latin women are being heard or not heard in regards to what is happening today?*
> *Right now so many of the conversations are black and white... where do we fall... where are we in these conversations? We're not all liberal, there are some that are conservative... How do we bring all that together, even among us... because we are all colonized.*
>
> —JADA PINKETT SMITH AND JUSTINA MACHADO, RED TABLE TALK[82]

I had plopped down on the leather sofa in our living room. The kids were still washing their hands after arriving home after school. I turned on the TV and flicked to the kids profile my husband had set up in our Netflix account. The kids and I are non-repentant binge-watchers, often leaving Dad to his coding and tech articles in the room next to us. And since my kids can resemble their mother, we inevitably dissect the series afterwards. On that day, we were getting close to the end of How to Train Your Dragon 2, and my son was already peppering me with questions about why the bad guy was so bad.

My phone vibrated with a message from my work wife. It was entitled "14 Things People Think are Fine to Say at Work—but Are Actually Racist, Sexist, or Offensive"[83] from *Business Insider*. The article defined microaggressions as "unconscious expressions of racism or sexism. They come out in seemingly innocuous comments by people who might be well-intentioned." The second paragraph went straight for it; "from telling a new female worker that she 'looks like a student' to asking a Black colleague about her natural hair, microaggressions often exist in the workplace, too. And they can make a workplace feel unsafe and toxic."

The article hit a nerve. Since I started my professional career, like many Latinos living abroad, my cultural identity has received unnecessary categorization. I have been told I am more Colombian because I am so "active" and likewise criticized for being "too American." If I claim my brownness, I get incredulous stares from White people, and if I say nothing, I pass as an Anglo-American, disclaiming my fellow sisters and brothers of color. In a meeting years ago when my accent unconsciously shifted, I received an outing response of "I love when you talk *all Miami*." Each time I felt the cut of unspoken cultural bias.

Only weeks before, my work wife Didi and I had gone for after-work beers. As a trilingual professional with the kind of inimitable charisma that comes from smarts, experience, an impeccable sense of diplomacy, and a striking, natural beauty, Didi was no stranger to double-edged compliments or subtle slights. We delved deeper into heavier topics of race, color, gender, and lookism while we sipped our beers and munched on a basket of chips. Insomnia had had me up the night before watching documentary shorts about precolonial African hairstyles as social indicators of family background, tribal affiliations, grief, going to war, and so forth.[84] I wondered aloud how this has influenced postcolonial Latino communities—hair being a significant cultural identifier in our communities and workplaces.

As we discussed how Afro-textured hair is commented on and controlled in the workplace, particularly in light of its deeper and painful historical context, I examined my own privileged position as a light-skinned Latina with straight hair. When Afro-Colombian journalist Mábel Lara received online criticism for wearing her hair curly on TV many years ago, I instantly applauded her, feeling pride in her claiming a part of identity; but I did not realize how truly revolutionary this act was against the daily pressure of a "classist society" which thinks "curly hair is tasteless," as Lara says.[85]

Touching a colleague's hair or barraging them with comments about their hairstyle changes ("Oh my God, I love how much you change your hair! Short then long. Is that a *weave*? I always wanted to try that!") is a show of exoticism that "others" the colleague, reminding them that they are seen as Black or Latino in the office. Mentally prohibiting those behaviors as social faux pas is simply not enough; it fails to understand how truly offensive such acts are, due to the historical context of identity and pride as well as the control and marginalization that African[86] sons and daughters have enjoyed and endured, respectively, through their hair. Moreover, these are the kind of behaviors in the office that are not only common but for which minorities are told, "Oh, I didn't mean anything by it. That was not my *intention*. You are too sensitive."

Discussing hair is only one small example of microaggressions against minorities at the workplace. At the office, we can be too quick to forget past oppression, thereby ignoring its modern-day consequences. Between the 16th and 19th centuries, about twelve million Africans were sold into the transatlantic slave trade. About 4%, or 400,000, were forced to go to the United States.[87] And of these people who were sold into slavery in the US, almost half came from the area surrounding the Senegal and Gambia Rivers and west-central Africa. When men (comprising about two-thirds of the captives) and women were abducted and sold, they would be stripped of their clothes and jewelry, and their heads were shaved. While women might be given more privileges to walk above the cargo haul, they were continually raped. The process was more than just inhumane transportation; it was a crushingly systematic stripping of personhood, identity, and dignity.

In Latin America, Spaniards and Portuguese men used the same mentality to colonize indigenous populations (as well as to introduce slaves and slavery) between the 15th and 18th centuries, up to the campaigns for independence in the 19th century. Millions of indigenous people were decimated through disease and violence that included the raping and subsequent births that inevitably crush and twist colonized communities. By some estimates, regional populations were reduced by as much as 90%, with other areas being left completely depopulated. The following is a description by Dominican Friar Bartolomé de las Casas in 1542:[88]

> After having killed not only all people of rank but almost all males capable of bearing arms, the Spaniards subjected the rest [of the natives] to devilish serfdom and exacted slaves

> *as tribute. Since the natives did own other slaves they had to hand their own sons and daughters. Shiploads of which were sent to Peru to be sold. Beyond this [the Spaniards] committed so many murderous deeds and atrocities that an entire kingdom...which had been one of the most populous and fertile on earth was utterly destroyed.*

As a daughter of a colonized country, having been brought up in another country that saw the rise and fall of slavery and continues to be plagued by intense racial tension, I could feel the difference speaking to Didi, who was raised by parents who grew up African in the country of their ancestors, relatively untouched by the horrors of the transatlantic slave trade. I recounted to Didi how hearing the loaded compliment of having "*pelo bueno*" or "good hair" made me realize how Latinos measured each other against a Eurocentric ideal. It felt like control, in a way I did not understand when I was growing up.

I brought the conversation back to the Americas, mentioning to Didi how I felt particularly moved by accounts of Black women being forced to cover their hair during the 1700s in Louisiana.[89] Jameelah Nasheed, writing for *Broadly* (*VICE*), sums it up nicely: "Yes, their hair was so damn beautiful that it was illegal." At the time, Creole women would arrange their naturally full and curly hair with gorgeous jewels and feathers. The attention they would attract in public was so disturbing to those who loathed to see these women overstep their "place," White society lobbied for a law that would prohibit such displays of Black female pride. Didi shook her head, saying, "You see. It's all about control, but identity is hard to totally control."

Women simply found ways to beautifully and elaborately cover their hair, so they ended up still spinning heads anyway.

The tignon law—named after the headdress required—was no longer in place by the time the United States purchased Louisiana in 1803. Perhaps not surprisingly, it was Black hair that supported the first Black female millionaire Madam C. J. Walker, who further developed the hot comb that had been invented by a French hairdresser during the 19th century as well as other hair-straightening products. Much later, during the 1960s and 1970s in the United States, wearing one's hair naturally became a symbol of resistance during the Black Pride movement.

Didi asked me if I had seen a recent story about an American child being forced to cut his hair by a school official. It felt like all the recent headlines were about how Black communities were being repressed and persecuted back home, including at the office and school. Professional and school dress codes might ban natural hair styles, such as locks and twists. Published in 1999, the children's book *Happy to Be Nappy* by bell hooks was such a revolutionary expression of pride in African hair as to have been covered in my women's literature class in universities.

We ordered another round, including a "panache," a cocktail of beer and soda popular in Switzerland and France. I stared blankly. Didi laughed at me, saying, "What? I know you don't think this is beer, but I'm taking my time." I giggled and made a self-deprecating joke before taking a deep breath and said, "*Aye, mi'ja*. Taking our time to discuss the effects of colonialism in the workplace." Didi laughed again, saying, "We have the best conversations. Did you like the article I sent you?" Didi asked. I nodded.

"It's good, right? Talking about discrimination in terms of microaggressions is critical for the work context," said Didi.

She mentioned an example of a faux compliment for a Black

or Brown colleague from another country: "You're so articulate." Recalling one of my first school trips from my predominantly Cuban-American high school in Miami to a northern state and receiving comments from mostly Anglo-American students at a scholastic competition about our ethnicities and accents, the comment resonated as one of those that stings more with time. "We (a white-dominant society) expect black folks to be less competent. And, speaking as a white person, when we register surprise at a black individual's articulateness, we also send the not-so-subtle message that that person is part of a group that we don't expect to see sitting at the table, taking on a leadership role."[90] Language is, of course, a huge issue among Latinos. In our places of work or our private spheres, we might receive the comment: "We speak English here."[91] With the proliferation of smartphones, videos of such encounters can go viral in a matter of hours, potentially affecting jobs and business reputations.

Another comment the article brought up is the dreaded mistaken identity issue ("You all look the same to me"), wherein a supervisor or coworker calls one employee by the name of another individual of the same ethnic or cultural background. Being called the name of another Latina might be laughed off at the watercooler later on, but it never is actually funny.

For women, microaggressive comments can relate to age, looks, experience, and profession. A seasoned wealth advisor from a private bank related a similar story to me. She is an elegantly dressed women with a striking hourglass figure. When she arrived to provide training for a group of all-male colleagues, she was greeted with an ambiguously aggressive comment along the lines of: "Huh, you don't look like I imagined." She gave the presentation nevertheless, but the comment stuck with her like an invisible thorn.

Microaggressive statements often hide behind the tone of a compliment or nonchalance, but their rub is in how they identify the recipient as different or "other" than the speaker because of racial, sexual, gender, and age biases. The article Didi had forwarded me listed a few:

- "You're transgender? Wow, you don't look like it at all."
- "Oh, you're gay? You should meet my friend Ann. She's gay, too!"
- "Where are you actually from?"
- "The way you've overcome your disability is so inspiring."
- "I think you're in the wrong room—this is the programmers' meeting."
- "Are you an intern? You look so young!"
- "Is that your real hair?"[92]

As the daughter of immigrants, I have heard at least half of those statements in one way or another. More often than not, a faux compliment will let me know a colleague sees me as an Anglo-American when I am on-the-clock and as a Latina after work. Every time, it cuts a little. Often, I do not even feel it immediately. My mind travels back to the conversation many hours later while I am having coffee or standing in the elevator. The comment then gets added to the jar of moments that is my relationship with that person, and as more jars fill, I realize they see me behind a cloudy wall of misperceptions.

The story of the people from my continent has, historically, been one of migration, and it continues to be so. The Economic Commission for Latin America and the Caribbean (ECLAC) reported in 2014 that about 28.5 million people born in Latin America and the Caribbean live outside the countries where they were born.[93] That is 4% of the total population in Latin America and the Caribbean and well over three times the population of my home now, Switzerland. According to the

ECLAC survey, about 70% of the total expats from Latin America and the Caribbean lived in the United States. In the United States, Latinos are now the largest minority, comprising almost 60 million of a population of roughly 330 million people.[94] Of course, there are complexities that are masked in the US census numbers. Latinos are directed away from the box *White alone, not Hispanic or Latino* without the same reflected in the *Black or African-American alone* option, meaning that the US census does not reflect the Afro-Latinx identity.

The thing about our identities as modern-day Latinos living outside our ancestral homelands is that they are often rooted in voluntary or traceable immigration, shaped by our language, food, national and regional histories, and some shared regional values that descended from the specific kind of colonization we went through, including religious. And because of the kind of colonization we went through, we have a broad spectrum of experiences and cultural values. This is ignored or overlooked in countries like the United States, where already-reductive discussions of race are often constricted to color or a mere handful of monolithic categories, without any appreciation for the inherent nuances.

These nuances also include prejudice within our communities, including colorism, a bias based on how light or dark one's skin color is as opposed to one's "race." I witnessed its biting grip for the first time as a teenager visiting family and friends in Colombia. Sitting in the back of an unairconditioned taxicab driven by a dark-skinned Colombian man, I was relating to a family member that someone close to me was pregnant. The young woman was unmarried and had not graduated from high school. The family member, an older woman with self-described indigenous features, asked me whether the father was Anglo-

American. I said I did not know but that I had heard that he might be Black American. Why? She replied immediately with disappointment, *"Aye, pero se tiene que mejorar la raza."*

I was stunned, looking at the driver's seat and praying the driver had not heard the comment. I felt slapped, like the first time I heard the term *spic* while my family was living in Central Florida. My sister had come home having been called the word, and we balked at it, confused, looking at the word like roadkill. And here sat next to me was a woman who might have been called that word saying that being whiter is better. Admonishments like "Don't stay out in the sun" and "Your hair looks better straightened" made more sense as the vicious and perverse irony of colorism in my own community.

As I recounted the story to Didi, she shook with resonance. Her eyes shot open when she heard what my family member had said, and she replied, "We have the same saying in French *'améliorer la race.'*" She knew what I meant instantly. Of course she did. Children of immigrants inhabit the same racial and cultural borderland, even if the names of our streets are different. At the end of our chips and beer a handful of years ago, my work wife and I felt closer than ever, sparking a friendship that has become a beacon in my professional and personal life.

A few months later, she invited me to a small get-together attended by other women with demanding careers. One of the younger women had just started a new career at a small NGO. With a newly minted master's degree, she was looking to make a good impression. She mused as to whether she might keep to herself and just get the job done. On one side of the table, the women agreed. Keep your head up and your name out of people's mouths, they said. On the other side of the table, Didi and I wondered if there was another way to approach making friends at an office where one is a (visible) minority. We pointed to our friendship as an opportunity to breed connection and network. I agreed. It was so easy for Latinas or Black or Asian women to keep to themselves, missing the opportunity to reach out to each other and share similar experiences. It is that kind of support that can get us through the tougher moments, and when necessary, the courage to report discriminatory behavior and to survive the aftermath of that report. It has been said that discrimination cannot stand the light of connection. Perhaps the same could be said for the effects of discrimination as well, we suggested.

On a different level, weight bias can be another source of discrimination in the workplace. In general, beauty bias can cost "less attractive" men and women 5% and 4% of their respective salaries, e.g., 230,000 USD over a lifetime. [95] Mirta is a plus-size woman of fluctuating weight and has encountered several unwelcome comments regarding her size. At a critical moment in her career, Mirta's supervisor made a comment to her that their director had a bias against her weight, as confirmed over movies and a drink with the HR manager. Mirta was devastated, thinking of the comment on a daily basis at work. The supervisor eventually apologized when Mirta confronted her a month later, but the damage was done. "Instead of protecting me from the discrimination by addressing it head on, she had extended it to me. Our relationship was never the same, and she never spoke of it again," said Mirta over coffee before starting her new job at a nonprofit dedicated to women's issues. Mirta is not alone, as one "Dear Prudence" advice column entitled "Help! I Think My Co-Worker's Weight Is Impeding Her Career. Should I Say Something?"[96] that features a querying manager wanting to help her overweight colleague "Claudia" shows:

For your part, promote Claudia's case to your directors on the strength of her work history; my guess is that you've never interfered with another colleague's personal life on the strength of your concern for their health, so you can safely dispense with that fiction. You say you want the best for her, so let me present you with your two options: 1) You try to find a "delicate" way to tell an excellent employee that the reason she's being kept back at work is because some of her superiors think her body is an unprofessional size, and that she can only be trusted with clients if she loses weight, or 2) advocate for people, especially women, in your company to be accorded raises based on the strength of their work and not their size. The second option is the best; please choose it.

The same goes for telling a colleague or candidate their gender, race, or sexual orientation is holding them back or the reason why they did not get the job. Instead of protecting them from discrimination, you are extending it. Sonya, a multilingual project manager, was told as much by a (female) hiring manager when she applied to work for a team that was composed predominantly of women. They wanted a man to balance out the team. "Hearing I didn't have the required skillset would have been better. But what am I supposed to do about being a woman?" she told me. A few months later she found another position, but she felt dejected for weeks after that incident.

Discrimination in the workplace has a steep price tag. In 2012, the Center for American Progress published[97] a report stating that discrimination cost American businesses a staggering 64 billion USD. The report defined discrimination by outlining that "employment discrimination can occur based on a host of characteristics that are completely divorced from an employee's performance on the job. These characteristics include an individual's race, color, ethnicity, sex, gender, age, disability, national origin, religion, veteran's status, or pregnancy status." Genetic or other health information can also be a basis for discrimination.

Researchers indicated that this loss represented the cost of losing and replacing more than two million American workers who leave their jobs due to unfairness or discrimination. According to one American business professor at Arizona State University, Jose Hom, the cost of replacing a departing employee can range between 93% and 200% of his or her salary. Another study calculated the cost at somewhere between 5,000 and 10,000 USD for an hourly worker and something like 75,000 USD to 211,000 USD for an executive who made an annual salary of 100,000 USD.[98] According to the World Bank,[99] in India the cost of discrimination amounts to somewhere between 0.1 and 1.7% of India's GDP. The preliminary study showed that the hundreds of millions of USD lost in unearned wages directly impacted the national economy.

Discrimination might cost business billions, but the individuals experiencing it can come to see it as an inescapable probability. In one study done by the American Center for Progress, researchers found that some 42% of gay individuals had experienced some form of discrimination at work—amounting to an enraging one-out-of-two chance of workplace discrimination. For transgender individuals, the number nearly doubles to 90%, including those who had experienced mistreatment or harassment or took action to hide who they were to avoid it. Within that 90%, almost 50% reported more extreme forms of discrimination, including employment termination, being denied employment, or not receiving a deserved promotion because of their gender identities.

What is even more frightening is the likelihood that a formal report will result negatively or, at best, in nothing. In the United States, the Equal Opportunity Commission and its state and local partners hear some 100,000 cases of gender, race, disability, and other discrimination cases yearly. Only 18% result in some kind of relief for the employee; for race-based complaints that number drops down to 15%, despite being the most commonly filed kind of case.[100] When one considers that many professionals may decide to "move on" despite the damage, these ratios are staggering.

Tonia felt the same kind of pressure to just "play along" as one of the few Black women in her office. A professional with a jawline that could cut any fashion magazine in half and a preference for formality and professional distance in the workplace, she had been invited to a performance review discussion with her boss that unexpectedly ended in sharp disappointment. She had met or exceeded her key performance indicators and received positive external evaluations from her clients; she expected a positive discussion. Her boss informed her that the rest of her team—all White Europeans, including him—had commented that she was "cold." Tonia was stunned. Yes, she tended to eat her lunch on her own, often spending the time to run errands or read *The Economist*. She preferred to keep her off-the-clock moments for her personal ends. Why did that matter? Others had their own personalities—some enjoyed a late lunch and many preferred to spend their lunch neverendingly criticizing the company and the leadership. She did not find this productive and wondered aloud how this affected her performance, showing her displeasure with the criticism.

"Then what could I do? I was the 'angry black woman,' and he stopped listening," she said. Had she been a man, her taciturn lunch tendencies might have been lauded as the mark of efficiency and professionalism. This was just the most recent in a continuing line of discussions begun by her boss several months prior. She was frustrated. Why was her preference for the use of her lunch break not considered a matter of personal choice? Why did she have to subject herself to that kind of negativity to show comradery with the group? She said she was a private person and wanted to be respected for keeping a strong professional boundary between her downtime and work time. But Black women are supposed to be always ingratiating and serviceable, right?

I thought about "mammy," the American characterization of a desexualized, matronly Black-American women who relished serving her White masters or employers. This was the mold Tonia's boss, a White French man, wanted to bend my friend into. With little options, she decided to start documenting everything for the moment she might have to take action. I wondered if documenting would make any difference if she was likely to be told, "Oh, you're too sensitive. I didn't mean it like that. It has nothing to do with you being Black." Without a platform to safely discuss these issues at work, they often stagnate in silence.

Unsurprisingly, Tonia quit her job as still others teeter on the edge of racial alienation and bias at work. Meanwhile, talent and money are wasted. Feeling like we cannot be ourselves at work can take a large toll on our mental health, and it is a price that many workers as well as companies are no longer willing to pay. Moreover, as more minorities vote with their time and their talent, discrimination is something that cannot be outrun or outperformed and can no longer be ignored by corporate leadership wishing to stay relevant.

CHAPTER SIX: DISCRIMINATION FOCUS ON THE MOTHERHOOD PENALTY AND FATHERHOOD BONUS DICHOTOMY

> *I have frequently been questioned, especially by women, of how I could reconcile family life with a scientific career. Well, it has not been easy.*
>
> —MARIE CURIE[101]

As a new mother, I could not wait to go back to work. I would seethe with jealousy thinking of all the people calmly listening to music and looking out the window on their way to the office. Whatever they were on their way to do, I was certain there was at least a chance someone would tell them "good job" or a gleeful "thanks." I read every "mommy blog" I could get my grubby water-retaining hands on, but no one's experience echoed mine. Everyone bemoaned having to go back to work after giving birth, as I was dutifully reminded by friends back home.

The International Labor Organization (ILO) Convention on Maternity Leave reckons that the period should be at least fourteen weeks.[102] In Geneva, where I live, maternity leave is sixteen weeks with 80% of one's salary paid by maternity leave insurance. This time frame certainly influenced my readiness to return to the office. There is a significant difference between having almost half a year to bond and recover and being forced to leave a week-old baby in the care of someone else while your body is still struggling to heal. Helpfully, across the world, over half of all countries offered at least fourteen weeks of paid maternity leave as of 2015 (a 17% increase from 1994), with paternity leave following suit.[103] Perhaps it was no wonder my experience was so different to my friends stateside, living in one of the few "developed" countries without federally mandated maternity leave.

Regardless of the length of maternity leave, returning, newly hired, and applicant mothers may find discrimination in the workplace, whether as regards promotions, recruitment, or salaries. Claire Cainne Miller of the *New York Times* wrote, "One of the worst career moves a woman can make is to have children."[104] That motherhood can hurt career and salaries while fatherhood can be a boon has sadly become common knowledge. Moreover, the motherhood penalty—the salary dock that comes with having kids—can be harshest on those mothers with an already low income and often minimally affects those in the top 5% earning bracket.

Unsurprisingly, the negative impact of motherhood on the salaries of women is not limited to the United States, where maternity leave regulation remains a challenge.[105] In a study looking at the "motherhood pay gap"—the difference in salaries between women with and without dependent children as well as the difference between mothers and fathers—the authors found that while the existence of a motherhood gap seems universal, the magnitude and duration of the effect motherhood has on wages varies from country to country. The gap appeared to be larger in developing countries than in developed countries, and factors including the number and gender of the children affected the gap. In many European countries, having only one child minimally affected the pay gap for mothers, whereas in developing countries, having girls (as opposed to boys) created the smallest pay gap, presumably as girls would be more likely to help in their mother's work in the long run. Longer maternity leave periods also tended to affect the pay gap.

Even when returning from a lengthy maternity leave, returning to the office can be a mixed bag, even for mothers like myself who relished the opportunity for a break from the much harder work of staying at home to care for a baby. I was happy to share a similar sense of relief with a new mom returning to the office, where breaks take on a new sense of luxury.

"Yeah, the bathrooms," said Mercedes, giggling. Best described as the adult-incarnation of the Antoine de Saint-Exupéry's the *Little Prince*,[106] Mercedes is the kind of person who would laugh self-deprecatingly while building a car from a matchbox. "I know, right? You've never appreciated the luxury of going to the bathroom by yourself or just stopping your work —without asking permission—and going to get a coffee to drink for fifteen uninterrupted minutes," I replied.

Just like I did, Mercedes felt almost guilty for enjoying her time at the office. I had been itching to go back to the office not only for the comradery but for the validation of my tangible performance results. Simply put, I missed the feedback and rewards that paid work can offer. Oddly enough, I received comments like "Oh, you can tell me the truth. I know how hard it is to be back at work. You would rather be at home," or "Oh, you work 100%. Poor baby must miss Mama." It was only after several months that I realized that those comments reflected much more on the speaker than on any lack or fault within me.[107]

In contrast, Joanne (the consultant who had moved to France) grew anxious before returning to work. Her husband would be staying with their firstborn while she started a new role, so she had the benefit of knowing he was bonding with their son. When her mind turned to her boys hanging out the whole workday together, however, she found herself missing them deeply. In speaking with her over a fruity black IPA, I reveled in our being able to express different experiences without fear of judgment or guilt. We were both ambitious, hardworking professionals—every bit in love with our families—enjoying each other's support while navigating motherhood.

In addition to sufficient maternity leave, having reliable childcare is critical to ensure the peace of mind workers needs to be fully productive. As new parents, my husband and I would receive daily updates about our baby's progress at our crèche—a full-time day-care center regulated by the local government, staffed by professionally trained caretakers, and led by a vibrant and caring Director. Meeting with the Director before we enrolled our first child helped to assuage our worries, as she assured us that she and her staff were a source of support for the parents as well. She addressed all our fears about missing important moments and the flexibility of the daily routine. Knowing that my baby was safe and well cared for allowed me to be fully present for my job and actually enjoy returning to the office.

In Switzerland, the proliferation of crèches has helped support the tripling of mothers in the workforce from the 1980s to the 2010s[108] (an astounding feat considering that women were only granted the right to vote nationally in 1971).[109] The trend of mothers entering the workforce does not end there. The US Bureau of Labor Statistics reported as of April 2018[110] that the labor force participation rate for married mothers was 68.6% and 76.5% for unmarried moms. Comparably, in Switzerland, 82.2% of women between the ages of twenty-five and fifty-four participate in the workforce, of which 70.2% are mothers with at least one child under six years.[111]

Pulling in data from the ILO, the ILOSTAT database, and the World Bank population estimates reveals that, as of September 2018, of the three billion workers across the globe, almost 40% were women. While the gender gap remains the highest in Northern and Western Africa and Southern Asia, 50% of working age women do paid work in comparison to 77% of their male counterparts. Nevertheless, when both paid and domestic work are considered, the "weaker" sex works longer hours than men, i.e., thirty minutes longer in developed countries and fifty minutes longer in developing countries.[112] Women with or without kids are the undeniable powerhouses of the world.

Despite the increasing percentages of women and mothers in the workforce, however, moms still make less money than their male counterparts, earning 70 to 90 cents on the dollar across the world.[113] The undeniable truth is that some employers still see moms as less reliable and more distracted at work. Sadly, I encountered this directly during an interview for a leadership position when the CEO of a small engineering firm questioned me at length about my children, their ages, and our childcare situation—unequivocally indicating that he considered my status as a mother relevant to the position. According to economist Laura Tyson, discrimination continues to play a key role, even when accounting for various other socioeconomic factors such as education and occupational choice:

> *Discrimination, stereotyping and implicit biases still play a role. Finally, and this is significant: even taking out the education effect, the occupation effect, the sector effect, the part-time work effect, and the motherhood and fatherhood effects, a gender gap in earnings remains. This gap is evidence of persistent discrimination, stereotyping and implicit biases in earnings and promotion opportunities for women. Government policies, legal protections, and changes in business practices, such as regular pay assessments of earnings by gender and pay transparency, are necessary to combat these sources of the gender gap in pay.[114]*

The longer mothers take going back to work can also have an adverse effect on their salaries and job prospects overall. It is enough to keep some mothers completely away from a paycheck during the child-rearing years. A vibrant, resilient woman, Grace has spent nigh on twenty years raising children, staying at home for the last decade of that after deciding that juggling childcare and an unfulfilling day job was no longer tenable. A tour-de-force in her family and community, she is a modern-day

Renaissance woman with a voracious appetite for new books, new recipes, and authentic connection.

What was the easiest part of staying home to raise her daughters? "Knowing that my girls would be taken care of and my house would be run exactly as I wanted it to be," said Grace. Her response had been exactly like my mother-in-law's response, despite their generational difference. Trained as a florist in her young adulthood, my mother-in-law had longed to stay at home to raise her children, relishing the independence and control of essentially being her own boss.

On the flipside, the hardest part of staying at home for Grace started with the lack of decent childcare options that had instigated her questioning whether to quit her job to stay home in the first place. Like many American women, she had a Hobson's choice between high day care fees, low-quality care, or staying at home.

Ultimately, Grace loved staying home and investing in the future of her children by tending to their growth attentively and meticulously. But it was endless. There are no immediate results, no key performance indicators, no benchmarks or bonuses. Moreover, she said, there was the ever-present feeling that society did not consider her time valuable. "Being a stay-at-home is no one's parameter for success," Grace said.

I was taken aback by her response. Peering across that artificial and noxious divide of "working mom" versus "stay-at-home mom," I have often wondered if the grass was greener on the other side, without knowing the hidden costs or daily slights. As Grace had said, how often is being a stay-at-home parent considered a laudable career choice? It can be the default, the least-worse alternative, or even a phase, but too seldomly is it seen—from a professional perspective—as an admired or even appreciated career choice. That is wrong. Considering the immense work, talent, and tireless, often unseen, dedication it takes to stay at home in order to parent and maintain a household (a multifunctional job valued by some surveys at 160,000 USD a year),[115] it is an unacceptable failure to ignore the talent and work of stay-at-home parents.

Driving home her point, Grace said, "No one ever tells little boys or girls in school that staying at home is a successful *career* path option. What's more, if you have great kids, you aren't sure it's really because of you." Astonished, I asked whether the patriarchy was truly so nasty as to pit stay-at-home moms against working moms, while making both feel inadequate.

The bias against parents who stay at home can be especially complex for men. After New Zealand Prime Minister Jacinda Arden joined a rarefied list of pregnant world leaders, her partner Clarke Gayford announced that he would be staying home full-time to care for their daughter. The importance of his decision was well described by a fellow stay-at-home father, John Adams, of the *Telegraph*:

> *If there's one thing the world needs, it's positive role models for fathers to look up to. And here we have a guy with a successful media career who is cutting right back on his workload in order to do the heavy lifting at home. [...] In so doing, he is carrying a torch for stay at home dads around the world.[116]*

The number of fathers who stay at home is increasing, e.g., two million more from 1989 to 2012 in the United States —accounting for 16% of all stay-at-home parents overall.[117] Moreover, creating a work environment for parents to work part-time can create a more inclusive and tolerant culture. A dad working part-time, Joaquin impressed his colleague when he stood up for a newly pregnant team member in a resource-planning meeting by challenging the assumption that the colleague would want to return part-time. "Why was there an assumption that [she] would return part-time? Maybe her husband would stay home part-time," he said, unknowingly predicting the future. I asked him later whether he enjoyed working part-time, mentioning that my husband had. A smile jumped to Joaquin's face as he recounted how greatly he enjoyed his weekly day off with his school-age children, teaching them and exploring the world together.

The National At-Home Dad Network in the United States estimates there are as many as seven million fathers who are primary caregivers. Nevertheless, only 39% of dads surveyed thought they were doing a "very good job" compared to 51% of moms. Clearly, there is room for the media and the workplace to support and appreciate dads who are primary caretakers. Paternity leave has to be included at the forefront of the discussion about workers' rights as does a change to the discourse that reflects fathers' position as integral caretakers instead of bumbling babysitters.

Moreover, the failure to recognize that staying at home to raise children requires transferable technical and soft skills makes it particularly difficult for any parent wishing to return to the office after an extended period away. Current wisdom dictates that if you are a returning parent, you are best served by showing how you have kept your skills current, explaining your motivation to return to the workforce, repositioning "weaknesses" as strengths, and evincing a healthy dose of patience.[118]

Having worked for years before moving from Europe to Asia for her husband's job, Sonya says it is easier said than done. After the disappointment of being shortlisted but rejected in lieu of a male candidate who was needed—in the hiring manager's words—to "balance out" the heavy female-tilt of the team, Sonya found a challenging job a few corners away from where she used to work. In the meantime, she went through several dead-end interviews, unknowingly competing with internal candidates earmarked for the positions.[119] Sonya explained her frustration, saying, "I'm sure it's just me. I just feel like I need to control everything. At home, I take on the responsibility for making healthy meals and making sure everyone's needs are met. But it doesn't matter how much I prepare for an interview or even my qualifications, it's out of my hands if they have someone else or another gender in mind." Having been warned she might not be chosen because of her extended absence (three years), she struggled to believe she was an attractive candidate despite being an energetic, multilingual project manager with a master's degree.

Confidence is a critical factor in terms of occupational choice and corresponding salaries and positions, especially in traditionally male-dominated industries.[120] In the United Kingdom, women account for only 14.4% of STEM (science, technology, engineering and mathematics) jobs as compared to the general fifty-fifty ratio in the overall workforce. It begs the unappetizing question: Are boys just smarter than girls? (And, by extension, does the motherhood penalty versus fatherhood bonus merely reflect that difference?)

A meta-analysis by the University of Bath looked at one hundred such gender-based studies. Crunching the numbers for over three million people, researchers found that girls actually did better than boys in primary school. Boys were able to keep pace by secondary school, although girls kept a slight advantage over boys in regard to complex problem-solving. That being said, despite their advantage in class and homework, girls lagged behind boys when it came to test-taking. If boys were not smarter than girls, were they merely better test-takers?

To answer that question, the Programme for International Student Assessment looked at math and reading test scores of over a quarter of a million fifteen-year-olds from over three dozen countries. On average, high-achieving boys did the equivalent of a half year of schooling better than their high-achieving female counterparts. However, when reported level of confidence versus anxiety toward mathematics was factored out, the difference disappeared. That lead the researchers to question if not only anxiety was a factor but whether this was influenced by national differences in gender equality culture. Unsurprisingly, they found that in countries like Norway, Sweden, and Iceland the gender gap disappeared or even reversed.

Even in Scandinavia, however, there was a gender gap in STEM occupations, despite scholastic equality. If intelligence and scholastic ability were not dissuading girls and women, what other factors were at play? A study[121] of 1,327 secondary school students in Sweden suggested that two big forces were at play: "social belongingness" and "self-efficacy." Social belongingness is the inclination to gravitate toward places where people are more like us. Social efficacy is the similar but separate belief that we do better in those respective domains. Both girls and boys scored high in self-efficacy related to HEED (health, elementary education, and domestic) spheres, but girls scored lower in self-efficacy in regard to STEM studies, regardless of actual aptitude. In other words, boys believed they could do anything but tended to follow other boys into STEM jobs, whereas girls tended to believe they would do better in HEED jobs and preferred to follow other women into these jobs.

The dual factors of self-efficacy and social belongingness help explain the intimidating effect of walking into a managers' meeting of mostly men and, subsequently, why some women feel dissuaded from taking management positions. Therefore, increasing and maintaining the number of women, in particular mothers, in STEM occupations (as with management positions) is unfortunately a chicken-and-egg challenge that involves change across society, media, the workplace, and the home.

For HR departments and leadership and middle managers wanting to attract more women and retain working mothers, it takes more than posting a template maternity leave policy and aspiring to gender equality.[122] It involves addressing and training to avoid maternity bias in hiring practices and performance reviews, including in how female applicants are spoken about and the questions they are asked. When numbers are provided about how many women are in management and across the companies, parenthood numbers should also be highlighted to ensure that discriminatory practices that affect parents are not being ignored. Mentorship programs pairing leaving and returning mothers (and fathers) that allow for time and safe spaces to discuss policies, practices, and experiences that can be measured against turnover and performance indicators can significantly impact the culture as well as numbers of a company.

Moreover, ensuring childcare options, whether it be by subsidy, creation, or flexibility in working hours can go miles from an employee's perspective and lead to retention rates.

There is, of course, no substitute for representation; seeing parents of young children, in particular working mothers in leadership positions and part-time fathers at all levels, creates the kind of environment that attracts others in similar positions and serves as critical proof of inclusivity. Ultimately, in the workplace, the creation of a diversity and inclusion program can be a critical piece of puzzle, but how can it be done right?

CHAPTER SEVEN: CORPORATE DIVERSITY AND INCLUSION PROGRAMS - A BLUNTED SWORD

> *When I'm sometimes asked when will there be enough [women on the Supreme Court]? And I say 'When there are nine.' People are shocked. But there'd been nine men, and nobody's ever raised a question about that.*
>
> —RUTH BADER GINSBURG[123]

Employers who permit toxic cultures and discriminatory practices are under pressure to change—not just from their employees, shareholders, and customers, but also from a digitally connected society wherein racial incidents, sexual harassment, or other predatory and discriminatory practices can quickly turn into hundreds of thousands lost on stock markets and store shelves, employment terminations, and reputational hits that are difficult to bounce back from. Moreover, more and more companies have recognized that a more diverse and inclusive workforce can mean more productivity and better results in the workplace. But getting there can include pitfalls as much as panaceas, regardless of whether you are in a management role or not.

Recognizing the Changed Landscape

American activist Tarana Burk started using the phrase "me too" as far back as 2006 to inspire a conversation about the prevalence of sexual harassment and sexual assault in the workplace. But it was not until Alyssa Milano[124] started using the hashtag #metoo from her Twitter account to galvanize the discussion about and investigation into the allegations of sexual assault and harassment by Hollywood producer Harvey Weinstein that the movement become not only viral but global.[125] Canadians used #moiaussi. In France, the hashtag #balancetonporc and songs like "balance ton quoi"[126] by Angele had men and women of different generations arguing about what was acceptable from men in the workplace and on the public street. Notwithstanding the polemic, France became the first country to penalize catcalling and sexual intimidation on the street.[127] The law went into effect in 2018 after a court sentenced a man who had catcalled a twenty-two-year-old student, threw an ashtray at her, and then punched her in the face after she remonstrated with him.

Harvard Business Review conducted a 250-person sexual harassment study between 2016 (before #metoo) and 2018 that suggested that while instances of sexual coercion (pressuring women into sex acts) and unwanted sexual attention (staring and unwanted touching)—the kind of behaviors "that drive many women out of their careers—might be declining, workplaces may be seeing a 'backlash effect,' or an increase in hostility toward women."[128] Despite 98%[129] of American companies having sexual harassment policies, stories of deeply embedded sexual harassment cultures at companies like Uber, Fox News, the US National Park Services,[130] and Sterling Jewelers[131] continue to plague headlines. Having a policy is simply not enough. The common link between these disparate companies is that sexual harassment was embedded in organizational culture, which can seem immutable, as we saw in Chapter 4: Toxic Work Culture: It Takes Just One Rotten Apple to Spoil the Barrel.

Another social movement driven by social media has been an increased focus on persisting racial tensions and bias. In the aftermath of the acquittal for Black-American teenager Trayvon Martin's 2012 shooting death, the Black Lives Matter movement[132] brought attention to the persistent inequities of Black people in the United States, especially in terms of police brutality and discrimination against Black boys and men. The Ferguson, Missouri, protests of 2014[133] brought the movement to global awareness with scenes of peaceful protestors being arrested and taken off city streets. The movement spread, and in 2016, protests were held in London, Berlin, Amsterdam, and the Netherlands, with supporters holding posters and banners bearing the well-known hashtag #BlackLivesMatter.[134] With the critical response[135] to the movement, discussions about national and ethnic identity became heated.[136]

This has been born out in my own Latin-American immigrant community, prompting some to ask, "When will brown lives matter[137]?" For undocumented Latinos, fear of retaliation and deportation has been silencing, not including the complexities of organizing a sector with intersecting educational, financial, sexual, social, and colorist[138] privilege and bias. Still, social media has allowed videotaped incidents to go viral, often ending in employment terminations and reprisals for the aggressors, such as when a customer yelled, "Get the fuck out of my country"[139] at a Spanish-speaking manager in a Mexican restaurant in Illinois; when a White lawyer threatened to call immigration authorities when he heard employees speaking Spanish to a customer; and when a White woman drove over a fourteen-year-old girl because she thought the girl was Mexican.[140] According to the Center for the Study of Hate and Extremism, there was a 176% increase in hate crimes against Latinos in the first two weeks after Donald Trump's election in 2016; a year later, the FBI would report that hate crimes against Latinos had risen by more than 24%.[141]

The changed landscape and need for increased diversity has also been highlighted in recent cases where fashion houses have gone terribly wrong, resulting in severe backlash and harm to their reputations, loss of sales and customer loyalty, and even product recalls. These include H&M's child's sweater advertisement featuring a Black boy wearing a green sweatshirt stating, *coolest monkey in the jungle,*[142] Prada's black-haired, chestnut-wood face with oversized red lips key chain,[143] and Gucci's wool balaclava jumper in black with a large red-lipped cutout for the mouth,[144] and Katy Perry's black loafers with red lips and large eyes[145] that conjure up hateful images of blackface.[146]

In the makeup industry, houses like Estée Lauder and Tarte have faced severe criticism for having extensive palettes for lighter skin and limited colors for darker shades.[147] Inversely, brands that heavily marketed to a wide range of skin colors and sizes, like the forty shades of makeup and extra-small to 3XL sizes available in Rihanna's beauty line, have received positive publicity and sales. Despite not being the first brand to cater to a more inclusive customer base, Fenty was one of the first fashion brands to make diversity a focal point.

Picking up on the trend, *Forbes*[148] noted, "There's no shortage of companies struggling with serving customers who don't cleanly fit into the 'mainstream' mold of a customer.[...] This missed opportunity on the part of a large number of brands has left the door wide open for companies who want to serve these customer groups." One such company includes Nubian Skin, a lingerie line founded by Ade Hassan, who was frustrated by not finding lingerie and hosiery that matched her skin color. Such companies not only hit an untapped market, they create "a mental and emotional transformation in these underserved customer groups and society at large. When brands say, 'I see you' to customers who are used to not being seen by the masses, the ripple effect of the impact goes far beyond where to swipe their credit card." Examples of this kind of transformational moment include the box-office record-breaking films *Coco, Black Panther,* and *Crazy Rich Asians*: "With all Latino, nearly all-Black, and all-Asian casts respectively, the movies injected a sense of pride in these audiences who have been grossly underrepresented in mainstream media."[149] Other companies have picked it up. Proctor & Gamble issued an ad series "The Talk" as a part of its "Black is Beautiful" community focus regarding the "talk" that Black parents in some countries have to have with their children about the racism they will face as they grow up,[150] as well as other conversations about diversity, including sexual orientation.

It is not surprising that many companies see diversity and inclusion programs as the answer to increasing diversity among employees and boosting inclusivity in their processes, products, and conversations, or as a tool to meet expectations from their customers, shareholders, or stakeholders. True diversity —the bringing together of different perspectives (because of inherently different lived experiences), can pick up missed markets or ideas, needs, or solutions. According to analyst Juliet Bourke, research[151] shows that diversity of thought can increase innovation by almost 20% and help reduce groupthink by 30%. Groupthink among demographically and experientially similar professionals is almost inevitable and can become institutionalized when unchallenged. People with different backgrounds will have different mental frameworks when it comes to problem-solving, especially as these affect experiences, people, processes, risk perception, and appetite, as well as previous solutions and foreseen outcomes. Organizations with inclusive cultures are twice as likely to meet or exceed financial targets, three times as likely to be high-performing, six times more likely to be innovative and agile, and eight times more likely to achieve better business outcomes.

Diversity and inclusion programs have become the rage among corporations looking for a quick fix; but are they fixing things, and if not, could they be better?

How Diversity and Inclusion Programs Have Failed

According to *Harvard Business Review*,[152] many companies have spent millions on diversity programs with minimal impact on numbers. There has not been the change in the last thirty years we might have expected. From 2003 to 2014, the percentage of Black male managers at commercial banks in the US went from 2.5% to 2.3%, for White women from 38% to 35%, and for Latinos from 4.7% to 5.7%. According to the US Equal Employment Opportunity Commission,[153] the ratio of Black men in management positions rose only slightly, from 3% to 3.38% in the thirty years from 1985 to 2016.[154] White women have seen their gains slipping in the same time, going from 22% of management positions up to 29% in 2000 and then losing ground by 2016 to 27.7%.

Considering that gains in diversity have been meager over the last three decades and that there is perhaps even a global trend backwards, there are many reasons why diversity initiatives fail. One of them includes overreliance on benchmarking tools, such as performance evaluations and review programs and tools, without the realization that bias can nonetheless creep in.[155] According to *Harvard Business Review*, some 90% of midsize and large American companies use performance ratings. Unfortunately, these can end up having either no benefit or a deleterious effect on diversity. For example, in some companies that implemented a performance review tool, no benefit was felt for Latinos and Black Americans, while a drop of 4% in management positions after a five-year period was felt for Anglo-American women.[156]

Moreover, retaliation is a real possibility. According to the US Equal Employment Opportunity Commission, 51.6% of all discrimination cases included a claim of retaliation in 2018.[157] Even when direct retaliation is not feared, obtaining evidence and support from others who may fear retaliation can still be tricky. When Mariluz's contract was not extended, in part due to her intention to become pregnant, she found it difficult to seriously entertain filing a formal grievance. Even after a member of her organization's gender equality ombudsman office passed by her office, noting her pregnancy and her upcoming contract conclusion, and asked if there was anything Mariluz wished to discuss, she concluded it best to say nothing. Her colleagues had indeed confirmed that the decision had been their director's and that he had included her desire to have a family as a reason not to extend her contract in a meeting witnessed by a handful of senior colleagues; but which of them would have served as a witness to his remarks in front of the ombudsman or an HR representative? Which one of them would have been the first to stick their neck out and risk their own contracts and promotion aspirations? Mariluz feared no one would, so she said nothing.

Moreover, Mariluz added, she did not want to put herself through the emotional turmoil of reporting the comment—right before having a baby. She poignantly said: "If I myself felt reticent to take action, I can imagine that hundreds or thousands of others feel the same way. How many cases are not filed?" What makes it worse for employees where there is an (unsuccessful) grievance procedure is that employers and managers may look away from any sort of complaint unless it is formally filed.[158]

Nevertheless, preventing discrimination based on gender, sex, and race must continue to be a priority for human resources department by *enforcing* zero-tolerance sexual harassment and anti-mobbing policies; taking on complaints with care, transparency, and neutrality; and educating staff on the complaints process, resources, and safe spaces as well as on bystander training. One key aspect must also be increasing representation of women, people of color, and LGTBQ people in management and key decision-making positions. Moreover, there remains a place for diversity and inclusion that does work.

Designing a Diversity and Inclusion Program that Actually Works

As we have examined, a critical area remains STEM work environments where women, Black Americans, and Latinos still account for less than 25% and 15%, respectively,[159] making successful diversity work programs in this area a particularly compelling example. One such successful program was at the University Corporation for Atmospheric Research, which is a federally funded institute that produces research and support scientists in the fields of atmospheric and earth sciences. Several key aspects borne out by the program include the importance of:[160]

- identifying an organizational diversity focal point;
- inviting interested colleagues into designated safe spaces to discuss diversity-related topics with an aim to building more inclusive teams and supporting diversity-related conversations, as well as to help identify programs and practices that could increase diversity;
- creating a diversity training program that examined issues such as power and privilege, gender, race, as well as a comprehensive bystander intervention training; and
- strengthening mentorship student outreach programs to support inclusive recruitment and retention strategies.

One hallmark of the success of the program has been its voluntary nature. When diversity programs are required or used punitively, they have been found to actually increase, not decrease, bias.[161] By focusing on inclusion and intervention instead of bias reduction, participants who see themselves as advocates of diversity can help to institutionalize desired behavior that leads to results by intervening when bias or harassment occurs and train people to talk about organizational diversity. This can lead to strengthened mentorship and student outreach programs that can support inclusive recruitment and retention strategies.

I mentioned the study to a former colleague, Diego, a White European male manager in his mid-thirties who recently inherited a small IT team featuring mostly men exactly like him, and I asked him about whether some of the learnings could help him in a particularly troublesome recruitment process he was managing. Immediately receptive, he was particularly struck by the importance of outreach programs but also highlighted the preparation of the terrain for the diversity of the team he might have in the future. For him, that meant ensuring that part-time work was something available to all employees and that scheduling systems able to accommodate variable hours would be put in place. Despite only a very small overall percentage of his department having part-time workers, he raised the issue of ensuring that the flexibility already existed to attract parents who might be interested in part-time work. When it came time to recruit for a new position, he was also the first person to approach his HR department with suggestions for using recruitment platforms sponsored by associations for women in IT. He asked whether HR had put aside a budget to support recruitment for more women and from underrepresented countries; his HR department was stunned. They had never considered it.

Diego added that, for him, another key element for creating a successful diversity and inclusion program was ensuring that inclusion was a cornerstone value that went beyond purely numerical objectives. Diversity programs that shove quotas or blind recruiting processes down the gullets of management without ensuring that inclusivity is encouraged and institutionalized can do more harm than good in his experience.

Another key element for diversity and inclusion programs to succeed depends on the buy-in and behavior of senior management, which can drive up to seventy percentage points of difference between the proportion of employees who feel included and those who do not.[162] Management that involves itself beyond the appointment of a focal point and one-off training sessions helps to make a diversity and inclusion program more sustainable. Such programs can express a core organizational value by institutionalizing tracking and reporting on key performance indicators and benchmarks as well as by implementing programs on a plan-do-check-act loop that allows for feedback, adjustments, and the acknowledgement of mistakes as well as success and follow-up.[163]

And then there is middle management. Often stuck between a rock and a hard place, middle managers can be forgotten when it comes to feedback, communication, training, and engagement—possibly derailing the entire diversity and inclusion effort. Underserved and overextended is the all-too-common fate of the middle manager. Providing them with more than just benchmarks but real evidence about how diversity and inclusion can perceptively impact their team's performance can be critical.[164]

Moreover, middle managers will inevitably have different profiles as facilitators, blockers, or bystanders. Senior leaders can help reach blockers and bystanders by modeling vulnerability through personal stories to demonstrate the difference between "equal" treatment that ignores systemic and internalized barriers or, worse, masks bias, and the kind of "equity" that can disarm, invite, and encourage. Such a strategy can provide more support to some employees until systemic barriers are removed so that all can have the same access; it can also expose middle managers to strong examples of counterstereotypes and high-performing, diverse teams.[165]

Ultimately, diversity and inclusion programs must start with a real (honest) look at the company and the behaviors and numbers it wants to change, eliminate, or elevate. A quick fix or a poorly designed program can do more harm than good, including through faulty grievance processes and bias backlash. According to *Harvard Business Review*, nearly half of midsize American firms and almost all Fortune 500 companies have mandatory diversity programs with varying degrees of success, some of which unfortunately operate to the detriment of diversity overall. [166] Reiterating the importance of having voluntary, experiential, inspiring, and practical training can raise awareness and create a shared language as well as a platform for continued conversations. This means seriously collecting and considering data regarding possible issues during the talent life cycle of employees (i.e., whether there are parts where bias has negatively impacted retention or development), identifying and continually tracking behavioral improvements, and focusing on establishing positive behavioral changes.

Work programs to help increase diversity that are voluntary and that feature mentorship and structured, measurable talent retention and recruitment strategies can make a substantial positive difference. This includes mentorship for (White, heterosexual) men and women in management positions who might be more reticent to reach out to interact with (other) women or other minorities. Ultimately, understanding why having a diverse team is a good thing, beyond the numbers and reputational effect, is key. There are countless corporate snafus that would have never happened had a woman or a Black person or gay individual been in the room, but there must also be an understanding that diversity and inclusion measurably boosts performance and well-being.

Diversity has great power in the work force, but it must be done right. The impetus must come from the top, facilitated by steady communication and a culture of respect. We have strength in our differences and so many opportunities to learn from each other. The first step is being honest with ourselves and recognizing our own biases. The second step is connection. Seeking out different approaches and different backgrounds can be a gold mine of support, information, and challenging insight into the organization as a whole, what it can be and become, and the community it serves. Finally, for those of us who benefit from diversity and inclusion programs, let us pick up the mantle where we can, offer constructive feedback, and offer our hands across the aisle to others. Every time we find the courage to be our true authentic selves, aware of and recognizing our differences, we bring more than our detractors could hope to understand. We not only belong, we make our world better, measurably and immeasurably.

SECTION 3: (WO)MAN UP AND BUILD YOUR ARMY

CHAPTER EIGHT: BEHIND EVERY GREAT (WO)MAN IS A GREAT WORK SPOUSE

> *I was so happy. Weirdly, I remember thinking, "My friend is here! My friend is here!" Even though things had been going great for me at the show, with Amy [Poehler] there, I felt less alone."*
>
> —TINA FEY[167]

You are almost at the office when your work phone buzzes in your back pocket with a new email notification. It is Monday, and you remember your boss left you a voice message late Friday. No time to listen now as you realize the black shoes you put on this morning belong to different pairs. "Please let me sneak in," you whisper to yourself as the elevator lights jump from number to number. The door pings open. "Please...," you start to say to yourself, and the sunlight obscures the face of the person standing behind the doors. You let out a big sigh, and your closest teammate knows in an instant what is wrong. He grabs you a coffee from the machine and takes you to a meeting room to calm down and take stock. A handful of minutes later, you walk toward your boss' office with a plan, feeling surefooted. Crisis averted, your trusted colleague smiles at the prospect of hearing about your win later over lunch. Nothing can improve a workday quite like a work spouse. Intentionally nurturing such a relationship can be the buoy we need to keep from drowning in the hours between nine and five.

In the second half of this book, we will start examining the things we can do to change the course of our work lives so that we can get (back) to where we want to be. Taking a work wife/husband, nurturing mentorship, and developing an entrepreneurial mindset are three critical ways we can ready ourselves to decide whether we are going to leave, lead, pray, or stay, as I will discuss in the last quarter of the book.

Authors of *Work Wife: The Power of Female Friendship to Drive Successful Businesses*,[168] entrepreneurs Erica Cerulo and Claire Mazur met each other when they were undergraduates and opened a successful e-business together only eight years later. They sold it in 2015 to Bed, Bath and Beyond.[169] When asked by *Fortune* magazine about what their greatest business accomplishment was, they replied, "Us!"[170] Since university, they had been fostering a close friendship that developed into a professional relationship built on trust, vulnerability, respect, and deep empathy—in other words, psychological safety. The authors consider themselves "work wives," reclaiming a term that dates back to the 1930s when "office wife" referred to a man's highly efficient secretary. Explaining their relationship, they wrote,[171] "It's a dynamic that requires an in-this-together attitude and approach that's viable in any business setting with right-minded people, and in our experience, it's a game-changing one."

In 2015, a Creighton University study[172] looked at responses from 269 work spouses in an open-ended online survey that culled from six different countries, including forty states in the US. The survey questions aimed at understanding the characteristics, management, and functions of a work-spouse relationship. The study's coauthors, Karla Bergen and Chad McBride, found—unsurprisingly—that the one characteristic that underpinned all work-spouse relationships was trust. In an interview with *CNBC Make It*, McBride stated that "trust comes from a history. It makes the workplace safe and it insinuates that the role of a work spouse is a constant one."[173]

In a toxic work environment, a strong work-spouse relationship can be the first front against demotivation, inefficiency, and quitting, as I learned early in my career. One year after stepping foot in Europe as a newly minted lawyer, a plucky American named Ana joined my team. "Hi, nice to meet you!" Ana said, her eyes sparkling. She had a small round face with oval spectacles, short reddish hair, and an exuberant smile. I was reluctantly polite, wary of how we would interact as the only Americans in the forty-person office—with me as the literary, psychoanalytic Latina and her as a science-oriented Midwestern Anglo-American. But Ana had killer smarts, a punch of sass, and a pinch of humble charm—an irresistible combination. It was not long before we became inseparable at the office—"work wives," without knowing the term.

Our offices were semiconnected, so it was easy to lob over a quick remark or question as we worked. At times, she would pass by my desk in the morning with two chocolate croissants to discuss the news or work; at others, I would invite her over for pizza to finish up work or to brainstorm before a big meeting. Hailing from different backgrounds, our diverse approaches (unified by our shared values of honesty, accuracy, hard work, and loyalty) created a sort of "team within a team" that was greater than the sum of its parts. Unsurprisingly, we started being assigned projects in tandem, which only augmented the ease and productivity of our cooperation as we started working essentially daily double shifts. Nevertheless, I was having a blast.[174] It felt like there was no problem too big for us to solve. Moreover, our friendship was like having family an ocean away from where we had grown up.

Inevitably, we both moved on; Ana relocated back to the States, and I stayed in Europe. Taking another job, I chalked up the productivity of our working relationship as something particular to our friendship, not realizing that those kinds of relationships are only available when sought out and nurtured. With more and more people sharing their office lives on social media, blogs, and other public spaces, our collective attention has turned toward the quality and quantity of our work relationships. According to a study in North America, 70% of business professionals report having a work spouse, compared to 65% in 2010 and 32% in 2006. Just like Ana and me, many work spouses discuss and share their lives broadly, dishing on everything from work and coworkers to current events and even their social lives, friends, and home lives. As further trust is gained in the context of these vital work relationships, individuals feel more comfortable discussing their personal lives, thus further cementing their trust and reliance on each other.

Moreover, having that kind of connection at work not only

supplies ready support in good and bad times; Bergen and McBride also found[175] it actually increases corporate loyalty and reinforces happiness in our romantic relationships. The logic is obvious: When we get our work worries off our chests before going home, we arrive lighter and present in our personal lives and feel better overall. Work spouses also directly help each other at work. Almost one out of three reported having done something to make their work spouses look good in front of their respective managers; nearly 20% were in superior-subordinate relationships (proving that not everyone hates their boss). Over 15% said they would occasionally do their work spouse's work for them. Despite this level of interaction and the fact that most work marriages are between opposite genders, very few work spouses reported being sexually attracted to or crossing the line with their work spouses. Moreover, as many as 40% reported that they did not spend time outside the office with their work spouse. Nevertheless, at the office, work spouses tend to stick together, to the extent that "fidelity" rates between work spouses are reported to be slightly higher than those among actual married couples.

The first time I heard the term *work wife* was from my friend and experienced manager, Robert, whom I mentioned in chapters 2 and 3 when discussing midlife crisis and being passed over at work. We were finishing up our quick work lunch when I asked Robert whether he and his partner had anything fun planned for the weekend. A social butterfly to Robert's sweet curmudgeon, Carl had made an immediately endearing impression on me as Robert's "plus-one" at a networking function. They did, but it was not what I expected. Robert had a stack of magazines, a good TV series, and an empty couch to look forward to, while Carl had plans with his work wife.

"Work wife?" I asked. Robert explained she was Carl's colleague and friend, who shared many similarities with Carl. They also enjoyed hanging out after office hours.

"They go dancing and brocanting together. It's perfect," said Robert. I remembered that I had seen social media photos of Carl at a party recently. "Oh yeah, they went clubbing. He had a ball. I watched *Downton Abbey* and went to bed early. It's really perfect. She is always willing to go out and do the social activities I can't be bothered with." I laughed and thought their relationship sounded wonderful. It was a perfect example of how like-minded work spouses can increase satisfaction at home as well as the office.

Work spouses are not only made from colleagues but also from friends, as when friends go into business with each other. Ben Cohen befriended Jerry Greenfield in the seventh grade as the two chubbiest kids in gym class. Later, when Jerry failed to make the cut for medical school and Ben's pottery business hit a wall, the two friends decided to go into business with each other. They figured they should do something related to the thing they had always loved to do together: eat. With only eight thousand bucks, they narrowed their choice to either bagels or ice cream, settling on the latter when it became the only affordable option. They gave everything to their business, sometimes working over one hundred hours a week and falling asleep on their refrigerators. Starting from their first ice cream shop in a renovated gasoline station, they would whip their business into a 300 million USD company. They experienced many ups and downs, including selling the company to Unilever and having to step down from the helm of the company. Through it all, the one critical constant was their friendship. "We chose to make our friendship the most important thing. The way we worked, whoever felt the most strongly about it got their way," says Cohen.[176]

Many have tried repeating the formula to varying success—for the business as much as the friendship. One such local success story in Geneva starts with a young entrepreneur and her popular indie coffee shop. Still under thirty years old when she first put her store sign on the window, Ilana has made her small business grow and thrive over the last five years. In the wee hours of the morning, she would open a bit earlier when she saw my family waiting outside for warm drinks and pastries on the occasional morning. Passing the storefront regularly, I would glance in and see Ilana refilling coffee for taciturn customers and dealing with bathroom emergencies or broken appliances, as her partner would whip up mouthwatering cheesecakes and salads in the back. Of course, being her own boss meant also being her own employee, so there is no escape from the menial work; but she always shows a friendly, determined face to her customers. When I asked her about some of the struggles that come with opening a business as a young woman in the (at-times) conservative city of Geneva, she smiled and looked at her partner. "We did it together," she said.

Picking up on the handcrafted beer trend, another intrepid Swiss local opened the doors in 2017 to an artisanal pub, alongside a beer geek friend. Heading over for a puckering sour or heady chocolate stout in their early days, my husband and I looked forward to being greeted by their delightful grumpy-old-men banter behind the counter. In a virtual game of bad cop/good cop, they complemented each other in terms of technical knowledge and experience with financials, the product, and the clientele. They parted ways sometime after their initial success, but it appears they have cemented a trend as more craft beer spots pop up in the neighborhood. Their story is not unusual when it comes to founding (and running) a small business.

Noah Wasserman of Harvard Business School found that only 16% of successful ventures were solo founded.[177] Instead of going it alone, the vast majority of entrepreneurs opened their business as a team of friends, family, or former colleagues. These partnerships, however, were not all equally successful. When friends and family cofounded, more than half of the businesses ended up failing, sometimes because one cofounder wanted out.[178] The sweet spot, it seemed, was collaborations between former coworkers. Wasserman proposed a reason for this distinction: Former coworkers were the most adept at having the hard conversations needed to carry a business through its lifespan, including changing initial understandings of how cooperation, investment, and returns work. Feeling like the relationship is a safe space for communication was key for a successful entrepreneurial relationship.

Collaborative work has become an inextricable feature of the modern workplace. Not only does the majority of the work we do in the office get done in teams, but according to *Harvard Business Review*,[179] employees can spend as much as three-fourths of the day communicating with their colleagues. Consequently, understanding how to work successfully in teams and fostering these conditions is critical for all of us, as well as our employers (and employees).

So, is there anything you should look for if you want to be a part of or create a high-performing team? Turns out there is, as Google discovered when it commissioned an internal study led by Julia Rozovsky.[180] Rozovsky focused on over 180 teams at Google, parsing out various data points based on background, preferences, and behaviors. She wondered if certain elements such as regular outside-of-work socializing, strictly following meeting agendas, or particular team composition (like combining high-credentialed or like-minded team members) would predict whether a team would perform well. It did not; teams with almost identical or opposite profiles and social behaviors could have wildly different productivity levels.

Undeterred, Rozovsky and her team shifted to analyzing "group norms"—the unwritten rules or codes that guide group behavior. After a year of looking at such group norms, like whether groups always or never interrupted each other or whether dominant personalities muted themselves and shy individuals came out of their shells to match the collective behavior, the researchers started to see patterns. But they did not know what was causing these behaviors. Rozovsky found a clue in a study[181] published in 2010 from Carnegie Mellon, MIT, and Union College that had analyzed the behavior of 699 individuals in a controlled study on group work. The psychologists found that while intelligence was not a strong predictor of group productivity, a shared sense of "social sensitivity" was. In other words, the most productive groups spent roughly equal time talking and were highly adept at detecting others' feelings through nonverbal cues, regardless of individual backgrounds and dispositions. A Harvard Business School professor, Amy Edmondson, in her study of 1999, called this shared sense of social sensitivity "psychological safety"— a "shared belief held by members of a team that the team is safe for interpersonal risk-taking," and further as, "a sense of confidence that the team will not embarrass, reject or punish someone for speaking up."[182]

For the Google researchers, this was the epiphany they were waiting for: Psychological safety was responsible for the pattern of behaviors they had found in high-performing teams. These were teams where members felt they could be open and vulnerable in sharing ideas without the fear of ridicule or reprise. They knew true agility and innovation because they felt safe enough to take risks, pivot, and repostulate—not just pay lip service to "failing fast." They were teams where individuals gave each other equal space to talk, listening to each other's verbal and nonverbal communication with interest and empathy.

You might be thinking that psychological safety as a precursor to performance is pretty obvious. I get it—of course we do better when we are not gripped by fear or *suspicion*. But how many of us ask about the behaviors that underpin psychological safety (like equal "mic time" or whether devices are put away during meetings) before joining a team or a company? Probably even fewer hiring managers and companies consider social sensitivity a key element in a new hire's profile, yet they can create a critical chain reaction by adding someone who could destroy a team's sense of psychological safety and consequently cripple performance. We can spend hundreds of thousands of dollars on the newest performance measurement tool and yet still fail to recognize the importance of fostering psychological safety and trust—the fulcrum of great work-spouse relationships.

The Minority Experience and Work Spouses

Having a great work wife and/or belonging to a trusting, high-performing team can take on particular importance for minorities or marginalized individuals in the workplace, who can carry a large psychological burden. In a statement that resonates with me as a Latina, Maura Cheeks states in an article entitled "The Psychic Stress of Being the Only Black Woman at Work,"

> *In the office, we're not really supposed to think about race, unless it's part of our job description. But for Black women, that's almost impossible. Being Black is a core part of our identity, and it colors the way we see the world and the way the world sees us. [...] Being Black and female at work means navigating insensitivities with dignity and assuming that most people are not ill-intentioned. [183]*

Despite constantly carrying our "otherness," minorities may feel we often meet silence or disbelief when we share our perspective on how inclusive the workplace *truly* is. This makes cultivating a work-spouse relationship with someone who understands that much more important, which I felt firsthand with the second and most recent work wife of my career, Didi. No strangers to that sense of otherness, both of us hail from an ethnicity and a culture that imparts privilege and one that receives prejudice. It is no wonder our discussions often gravitate toward geopolitics and intersectionalism. She is still the first person I ring up when I am happy or hurt, like when I am on the receiving end of discriminatory behavior and microaggressions, like: "You don't look Colombian. Come on, you don't feel White American?" or, "You're too American. Why do you attract so much attention to yourself?" or "Your English is so good. How are you Colombian?" A favorite was when an interviewer brought up the "disconnect" between my last name, language, appearance, and ethnicity.

One moment typified the kind of workplace mentality that alienates minorities and that a strong work spouse like Didi can help build resilience against. A few years ago, I was in a Swiss employment law training attended by forty or so individuals. Glancing around, I saw no indication that anyone hailed from outside of Europe (despite the number of international organizations represented). Most of the HR professionals were White French and Swiss women, and, unsurprisingly, the conversation about discrimination centered around ensuring equal treatment between genders. During lunch, I mentioned I was disappointed that we were failing to discuss the impact of racial discrimination in Switzerland and that, even at the level of civil law, the emphasis on gender discrimination seemed to exclude other vulnerable groups, such as those based on race, religion, age, or sexual orientation.[184] One of the attendees (let us call her Brigette) put down her fork, looked me squarely in the face, and flatly refuted my assertion that racism was an issue in our local job market.

Interestingly, Brigette was one of the most vocal and seasoned of the human resources managers and was taking the training as a "light refresher." During the morning's discussion about maternity leave protection under Swiss law, it was she who had sent ripples of silent discomfort when she volunteered anecdotes about women who had been fired[185] and, in her mind, gotten pregnant merely to "keep themselves on the payroll."

I was not surprised that my comment about racial discrimination pricked her. I suggested that privilege might be a reason some of us had not seen how racism affects our colleagues and neighbors and offered a few anecdotes. She shook her head no at each case until I recounted the experience of one of my French-Congolese friends, who speaks with a perfect Parisian accent and has a rare last name not easily identified as African. When she arrived for an in-person interview with a potential employer after passing the interview-by-telephone stage, the receptionist was surprised, asking "Are you really Fleur?" This reaction was duplicated by the interviewer, who double-checked Fleur's file, identifying her as a French national, and shrugged her shoulders. Fleur could not shake the feeling, echoed by other Black friends in Paris, that she did not look like the vast majority of candidates, a reality that was confirmed when she became the sole Black person in her new office. At that point in my story, Brigette hung her head. "Oh, well, that's different."

I later rehashed the conversation with Didi. Why had my biased lunchmate finally agreed that the reactions of Fleur's new employer's receptionist and interviewer were wrong? Without skipping a beat, she said, "It's because Fleur was French. She did not appreciate that behavior against a fellow French woman," implying if Fleur had been Congolese *only*, my lunchmate's reaction would have likely been less understanding. It was the difference between *self* and *other*, which is at the heart of bias against minorities in the workplace. Gay and lesbian friends stay in the closet at work, preferring to avoid unwanted bias or attention to their personal lives. Moms and would-be moms follow self-imposed rules forbidding any talk (or showing any photographs) about pregnancy or motherhood in the office. Children of immigrants and Black-American colleagues code-switch between their home languages and the crisp diction that signals to their White counterparts that they are nonthreatening. A work husband or wife can be a buoy in a sea of isolation, giving us—especially minorities—a safe space to be our authentic selves even if only for short periods of time.

Unfortunately, many of us cannot impact our work

environments to push for real cultural change in the office. It must come from the top. For leaders and HR, fostering a culture that boosts psychological safety in the workplace, teams, and relationships like work spouses is an irreplaceable component of improving and maintaining high levels of performance. And for the rest of us? We can seek and foster positive relationships that reinforce the feelings of safety in our teams and invest time and energy in close professional relationships that boost our well-being and sense of connection at the office—whether or not we call these people our work wife or husband.

Just like Erica and Claire and Ben and Jerry, these relationships can be the foundation of great work relationships, a business, or even a movement. The power of being intentional about these relationships is that we give them value instead of telling ourselves that we are wasting time on coffee breaks or friendly lunches. In other words, the time that we spend in meaningful work partnerships—often off-the-clock—is like the morning workout that warms our bodies even after the weights have been racked and the towels, thrown to wash. Our performance improves, and our personal satisfaction increases.

For women and minorities, forging these close professional friendships is a critical element for our career success that we often overlook. The story does not end there, however. Mentorship takes many of the same aspects of a work-spouse relationship—the trust and safety—and transposes these into guidance.

CHAPTER NINE: MENTORSHIP—THE SECRET INGREDIENT TO A GREAT CAREER

> *A mentor is someone who allows you to see the higher part of yourself when sometimes it becomes hidden to your own view. [...] Nobody has made it alone. And we are all mentors to people even when we don't know it.*
>
> —OPRAH WINFREY[186]

During university and in the early years of my career, meaningful mentorship seemed like a mysterious experience locked away in a secret garden of connection and inspiration. Since leaving Miami, I have yet to find a mentor who resembles me, a powerful representation of what I could be —something my classmates and colleagues of other ethnicities and backgrounds could take for granted. I have imagined a smart, ambitious Latina with a ready laugh and a contagious sense of courage standing on the other side of the wall, waiting for me. A community leader and a resource to other attorneys, she would exude love and pride in herself, her people, and her work. Closing my eyes, I imagine meeting her for coffee or a glass of wine; she would nod knowingly when I tell her about microaggressions in the office and tell me how she overcame the same. Maybe I would even work for her, hoping that I deserved the guidance she freely and generously offered. In my imagination, however, she has remained as I have increasingly understood the importance of mentorship for career growth and satisfaction, especially for the ambitious, young, and Brown.

A business phenomenon of the early aughts, Mark Zuckerberg attributes crucial moves in the life of running Facebook to the mentoring he has received, e.g., when Steve Jobs offered him advice on whether to accept early buy-out offers.[187] Of Jobs' advice, Zuckerberg said:

Early on in our history when things weren't really going well—we had hit a tough patch and a lot of people wanted to buy Facebook—I went and I met with Steve Jobs, and he said that to reconnect with what I believed was the mission of the company, I should go visit this temple in India that he had gone to early in the evolution of Apple, when he was thinking about what he wanted his vision of the future to be.[188]

Jobs is quoted as having had a powerful experience on his mission of self-reflection in India: "The people in the Indian countryside don't use their intellect like we[189] do, they use their intuition instead...Intuition is a very powerful thing, more powerful than intellect, in my opinion. That's had a big impact on my work."[190] Ultimately, what had worked for Jobs also worked for Zuckerberg—Zuckerberg followed his intuition and stayed the course, bridging the gap of youth and inexperience by listening to his mentor. He is not alone. Jobs himself was mentored by colleague and early Apple investor Mike Markkula, as Larry Page and Sergey Brin of Google were mentored by Eric Schmidt.[191]

Job's advice illustrates a subtle reason why mentorship can be so pivotal. It relates to the quality of information from a trusted mentor versus what is expressed in books and media. Since many authors and colleagues decide to keep sensitive or controversial experiences to themselves, some experiences (especially regarding hardship and discrimination) can only be obtained through a trusted mentor-mentee relationship. So, if the need and want is there, why is it so hard to find mentors? *girlboss* contributor Deena Drewis outlined[192] the polemic, citing a 2011 LinkedIn survey of nearly one thousand American women. While 82% believed that having a mentor would be important for their career development, more than half said they could not find an appropriate mentor. Twenty percent of polled women had never had a mentor at all. Things get even trickier depending on your profession; if you are a Latina lawyer like me, we are only 1.3% of all legal professionals in the United States.[193]

For women of color, finding a mentor can be particularly delicate. A significant reason is that Black and Latin women collectively comprise a small percentage of people in management positions. Despite comprising about one-third of the American population, Black women and Latinas occupy only 12% of management positions and 3% of Fortune 500 boards, explains Drewis:

And as with the gender pay gap, in which black and Latina

women make significantly less than their white female counterparts, women of color have it tougher—in no small part because they see less representation in the leadership roles generally sought out for mentorship.[194]

The last time I was in an environment with Latinas in power was back in my teenage years, after my family moved to Miami. My high school was over 98% Latina, including many of the teachers. Unlike me, many of them had been born in Miami, growing up without the feeling of being racial minorities, as they were surrounded by Cuban restaurants, dance clubs, Spanish-speaking churches, and wealthy property-owning relatives. This gave many of my classmates an inherent confidence about their identity that I have seen throughout their adulthood, never having needed to apologize for the borderland they inhabited. It is the kind of confidence I have met in South and Central Americans and Africans who grew up in cities where they felt included, distinguishing themselves by education and socioeconomic class.

Latina role models in English-language media and public life were few and far between when I was growing up in Virginia in the eighties, but things would slowly start to change.[195] I realized this on May 26, 2009, when hope slapped me awake with one headline: The first Latina/o and only third female member in over two centuries had been confirmed to the US Supreme Court. Her name was Sonia Sotomayor, and, finally, someone who looked like me held the most venerated seat of my profession. Moreover, her journey from a low-income Spanish-speaking neighborhood in New York to the upper echelons of legal practice belied a uniquely Latino and immigrant experience. In the presence of Sotomayor's mother,

President Barack Obama introduced Sotomayor's "extraordinary journey,"[196] saying that her Puerto Rican father, who had never exceeded a third-grade education, had passed away while Sotomayor was nine, leaving her mother to raise Sotomayor with a fierce love of education and community service. To wit, they had owned the neighborhood's only set of encyclopedias. I was ecstatic when she published her memoir, *My Beloved World*,[197] a handful of years later.

As expected, Sotomayor had excelled in school, pushing herself through private schools before landing a spot at Princeton University and then Yale Law School, but I was particularly moved by reading that her reaction to being surrounded by the children of privileged educations was to catch up over summers, devouring classics that her classmates had read in high school while she volunteered relentlessly, connecting to other Puerto Rican and Latinx students when she could. Her relationship to her community was pivotal in shaping her education and career. She recounts the experience of meeting Yale's General Counsel, José Alberto Cabranes, who would go on to become a well-respected judge and who very nearly became the first Latino on the Supreme Court himself. In her own words, he was everything she aspired to be—an ambitious and productive attorney serving his community:

> *When a young person, even a gifted one, grows up without proximate living examples of what she may aspire to become —whether lawyer, scientist, artist, or leader in any realm— her goal remains abstract. Such models as appear in books or on the news, however inspiring or revered, are ultimately too remote to be real, let alone influential. But a role model in the flesh provides more than inspiration; his or her very existence*

is confirmation of possibilities one may have every reason to doubt, saying, 'Yes, someone like me can do this.'[198]

Reading Sotomayor's words above, "a role model in the flesh provides more than inspiration, his or her very existence is confirmation of [...] 'Yes, someone like me can do this,'" I felt joy but also jealousy. During my law school years, there were only a handful[199] of other Latinos in my class and certainly no professors or administrators. Where was my Sotomayor or Cabranes? It is hard to tell looking back if I simply did not look hard enough in my community or whether my disappointment was inevitable. Regardless, I was very much aware that while Atlanta had a robust Black professional community, the Latinos were sorely lacking. I felt this in obvious and subtle ways. I placed as a top ten oralist in the regional appellate trial competition. I had done well, but I had missed the mark on an important issue. I gesticulated too much for the judges, who were predominantly White men from Georgia. I was told I would perhaps fit in with New York judges but not Southern ones, because I talked with my hands and moved my shoulders, head, and neck more than the staid behavioral habits of Georgia court lawyers. It was a small moment perhaps, but it was a poignant first for me as a law student. My cultural difference had cost me points. It would not be the last of such occurrences, sadly. Would my delivery (and overall performance) have been perceived differently had the panel consisted of female Latinas (or broadly, more people of color)?

There is such power in representation among our superiors, teachers, and mentors. They can read our cultural cues without distraction or marginalization. Just like in school, representation at the office can mean determining what behaviors, relationships, or decisions can serve us and those that can hurt us, while still remaining true to our identities. The difficulty is, of course, breaking into certain circles precisely when one is different. So, mentorship options for minorities can be limited. Seeking out younger or more inexperienced mentors who are on the cusp of becoming or have recently become managers becomes the only option.

One of the very few Latina managers I have worked with, Mercedes (from Chapter 6: Discrimination Focus on the Motherhood Penalty and Fatherhood Bonus Dichotomy) is a light-skinned Latina who has lived in Europe and South America. I asked her whether she had ever worked for a Latina and was not surprised that her answer was negative. She had barely known Latinas in power in the workplace. When she sought advice on handling an issue in her team or questions about promotions, she sought out her male and female peers, most of whom were European. Her answer was one of the first conversations hinting at a common path for minorities in the workplace: Find mentorship where you can, regardless of demographic. Now she stands as mentor for other Latinas as someone who works hard to maintain and expand her network. Mercedes has become a leader who stands out for being authentic while easily code-switching when necessary, but what about others who find it harder to adapt or visibly blend in?

Over tacos and margaritas, I asked a handful of friends —professionals in public and private organizations with experience working on various continents—what they thought about the difficulty and importance of finding mentorship for women, especially women of color. Victor, a Nigerian analyst with an entrepreneurial spirit and a ready ear, opened by saying he had not realized how often women self-censor and the effects it has on leadership and cooperation in the workplace. A colleague had opened his eyes when she pointed out how she was treated in the boardroom. He had never noticed it before, but when he started considering the interplay, he was able to personally confirm that she would often be ignored or challenged. Like many women, Victor's colleague slowly began to speak less during meetings and wound up conforming to the typical stereotype—a woman who did not lean in at the table. The vulnerability and openness of his colleague had sensitized him to an experience that his privilege of being an able-bodied man had not.

Listening sympathetically and analytically, Dante interjected, "But sometimes it's hard to promote women. It's a tightrope walk between encouraging them to speak in a meeting and inadvertently undermining them in the same fell swoop." A European living outside his natal country, he leads an IT team in a field where women are still few. He considered diversity in the workplace to be essential—not a "nice-to-have." That being said, he noted that few resources were afforded managers on how to mentor minorities, including women. Our dinner discussion was a rare opportunity for him to hear different unvarnished perspectives without the intimidation of working for the same company or boss. There is no easy answer to solving the lack of mentorship opportunities for women, but starting a dialogue with men and women in positions of power is an important step to changing the status quo. It also involves a leap of faith. It can be hard for us to imagine life outside our own experience, but believing and respecting the voices of minorities is an essential step. Moreover, the more voices that are given to the experience of women walking the path of leadership, the easier it will be to find bridges for all of us.

But speaking up as a woman has not always been easy. We are more likely to be interrupted (men interrupt women 33% more than women interrupt men),[200] are given less credence, are considered less suitable as leaders,[201] and are perceived as more aggressive when we do stick to our guns.[202] Speaking up yet being unheard or misunderstand or choosing the path of less resistance toward silence and acquiescence can feel like a Hobson's choice. In 2017, the *New York Times*[203] invited women to chime in on the phenomenon. "I can't even count the number of times I've witnessed a woman being interrupted and talked over by a man, only to hear him later repeat the same ideas she was trying to put forward," said one Grace Ellis. "I'd say I see this happen…two to three times a week? At least?"

For those of us frustrated by the silencing treatment of women in the office, we are no less frustrated by solutions that sound an awful lot like *just try harder*. Michelle Obama expressed a similar sentiment in an interview[204] with *The Cut* during the *Becoming*[205] tour: "And it's not always enough to lean in, because that shit doesn't work all the time." Author of the book that made leaning in synonymous with women making themselves heard, Sheryl Sandberg herself admitted that it was difficult to lean in as a single mom after the death of her husband:[206]

> *In Lean In, I emphasized how critical a loving and supportive partner can be [...]. Some people felt that I did not spend enough time writing about the difficulties women face when they have an unsupportive partner or no partner at all. They were right.*

Moreover, as an educated, heterosexual, able-bodied Anglo-American woman, Sandberg is susceptible to missing the realities that block other minorities from leaning in, further amplifying the need for mentorship and networking among women and minorities. Women of all racial backgrounds need each other—regardless of where each one of us is on her journey. Writing each other off as not "woke enough" only hurts our attempts at alliance, communication, and enlightenment.

Wishing to relive the frankness of my mentorship discussion over tacos and margaritas with Victor and Dante, I asked Dante's partner Ilaria whether she had had an influential mentor in her life. "Yes, absolutely!" An über-competent, results-driven, and strikingly attractive green-eyed Italian woman who combines joy and precision in equal measure, Ilaria exuberantly offered to talk to me about it over lunch a few weeks later.

We ordered our kebabs and fries as she started to explain. Before I had turned to the topic, she asked me whether I believed mentors could be hired. I had read about professional coaching, a route preferred by some new managers, directors, and even CEOs. A 2013 Stanford University executive coaching survey[207] stated that the two areas that board directors felt their CEOs needed the most improvement were "mentoring skills/developing internal talent" and "sharing leadership/delegation skills." Seventy-eight percent of CEOs who were receiving executive coaching for themselves said the decision had been based on their own initiative, while some 21% said that their board chairman had suggested it. Interestingly, 43% of CEOs rated "conflict management skills" as the most important topic for their personal development. Many of them had hired professional coaches.

Ilaria listened intently, wondering about the corporate application of what had been for her a deeply personal experience. I suggested that transformative mentorship, regardless of its inception, must be built on intimacy and trust; she instantly agreed. Her first mentor had been her childhood piano teacher in Italy. Ilaria's eyes sparkled as she spoke of her deep regret that she had never told her teacher how meaningful her example was. "She was my piano teacher from the time I was five until I was twenty. She was driven. Clear. Strong. She was a powerful representation of what I could be."

Ilaria's last four words resonated with me, as Supreme Court Justice Sotomayor's words had when she had written about her mentors. Representation is a powerful thing. Ever waiting for the first Latina/o for President of the United States, I instantly understood the effect on young Black boys and girls when Barack Obama was elected—children like five-year-old Jacob Philadelphia. The son of Carlton Philadelphia, a National Security Council staffer who took his family to visit the President at the end of a two-year stint, was so impressed by the first Black American President that his choice of what to ask the President was whether Obama's hair was like his own.

Without missing a beat, the empathic President replied, "Touch it, dude!" and bent down before the little boy. White House photographer Pete Souza's print of the moment that Jacob patted the President's head in a moment of humility and identification became instantly iconic. Speaking of the photo's significance, Carlton Philadelphia said, "It's important for black children to see a black man as president. You can believe that any position is possible to achieve if you see a black person in it."[208] I was recently reminded of how powerful Obama's image remains globally when I noticed one of his 2008 campaign posters on the walls of my progressive Swiss neighborhood. Like Ilaria had said, nothing replaces the power of an image that shows *what I could be*.

The power of trailblazers to make us believe we can walk in their footsteps has been something that industries outside the corporate world have long understood. If we call mentorship by another name, *apprenticeship*, we realize it is as old as professional life itself. A review of literature about mentorship in the South African construction industry focused on the transformative nature of mentorship in the face of rapid technological and education advancement, increased competition and workforce diversity, and high turnover rates.[209]

Unsurprisingly, pairing aging workers with younger ones ensured a transfer of knowledge and problem-solving skills that could greatly increase efficiency, reduce costly accidents and errors, and importantly, positively impact job satisfaction and retention rates. Interestingly, the researchers found that the "psychological support function" of the mentoring programs was merely one pillar responsible for upholding such positive results. Mentorship was powerful also for its role modeling and direct career development aspects.

The concept of apprenticeship in craft and manual work may be as old as these trades themselves, but how does the concept of mentorship fit into white-collar jobs, some of which may be entirely different from one technological generation to the next?

Several large companies have instituted corporate mentorship programs.[210] An article on the job platform Monster.com mentions that companies like Deloitte, Sodexo, Time Warner Cable, Caterpillar, Intel, General Electric, KPMG, Boeing, and Liberty Mutual all boast formal mentorship programs. The programs themselves vary widely. Some focus on matching new hires with more experienced managers and other colleagues, while some may be more tailor-made, with clear objectives for a specified time of mentorship, or enable their employees to rotate through different departments to gain different skills and knowledge.

Deloitte reported having a mentorship program called the Emerging Leaders Development Program (ELDP),[211] which aims to answer the question Dante had mentioned during our dinner conversation: "How can we effectively mentor minority colleagues?" The ELDP boasts of being a comprehensive, multidisciplinary program aimed at high-performing minority managers and senior managers. The aim is to help prepare them for positive career progression by using targeted skill-building sessions, self-assessments, 360° feedback, and one-on-one external coaching. The program features several specific modules, including dealing with unconscious bias in the workplace. Finally, the mentees are assigned with mentors who commit at least two years to their protégés to help drive their careers. Good examples of "talking the talk" for corporate mentorship programs are unfortunately no guarantee of whether companies actually "walk the walk." Few publish any evaluations of their programs' statistical or otherwise tangible results.

From our discussion of corporate mentorship programs, Ilaria turned the conversation back to her piano teacher. The real magic of her mentorship had been her conveyance to Ilaria that she had the power to do whatever Ilaria wanted with her life. "The sky is the limit—not in in terms of freedom but in terms of achievement. Many people put limits on themselves like, 'I could never be an astronaut,'" said Ilaria, "but this may be a lie." Another example had been a former supervisor, a no-nonsense, technically adept woman who constantly proved herself in meetings full of men. She was of the generation that had to choose among children, career, and marriage. The popular adage during her heyday was that women could only successfully manage two at a time, without utterly failing at all.

I once worked for a paralegal in Florida just like that, a woman who could be caustic but über-efficient and should have probably been a lawyer herself. She took me under her wing when I worked in the small general practitioner's office. On my birthday, she had taken me to buy suits for law school so that I would be prepared for interviews. She was the first (and still one of the few) woman in the legal field to outwardly support me and believe in me. It instilled in me an incredible sense of belongingness before I started law school, a feeling that stayed with me for the beginning weeks and months.

Ilaria continued. It was in her conversations with her boss, someone whose time Ilaria treated preciously, that Ilaria realized that she wanted to move further into her field and head her unit. Nowadays, Ilaria provides counseling to others. Above all, she treats her mentorship relationships intentionally, ensuring that time is not wasted and that growth is always the focus of the conversation.

Longing to explore this kind of supervisor-supervisee mentorship, I called up one of my confreres, José Ángel. After goading me for not having called in almost three years, we sat down to a plat du jour at a Spanish restaurant tucked away on a bustling street. We ordered the paella, and I asked him to tell me about his great mentors. He spoke of a senior partner at his firm—a man he felt he could trust with the keys to his very house. José Ángel had introduced me to him once, and I had immediately felt the authority he commanded. When he learned I spoke Spanish, he suggested I work on a case involving

South American parties. The senior partner's knee-jerk reaction to put my skills to use impressed me and evinced the firm's longstanding commitment to mentoring young lawyers.

Given this track record, I asked José Ángel what he looked for in a mentor-mentee relationship. He responded that there were two key ingredients to a great mentorship relationship. One, both sides needed to be comfortable with being challenged. Challenging staid perspectives or naïve convictions is pivotal, he said. He regularly sought out young apprentice lawyers who could think outside the box and were unafraid to voice their opinions. After two decades of lawyering, a good challenge for José Ángel felt not only refreshing but enriching. Two, there had to be an element of trust or even faith—a mix of respect and courage. The latter is, of course, much harder to find; but when it's present, it must be intentionally cultivated. For José Ángel, his mentorship relationships have not only opened doors for him as a partner in his law firm, they have also continued to motivate and enlighten him.

It was the kind of support that bolstered José Ángel when he faced prejudice as a new lawyer. He recounted appearing in front of a judge who took one look at his last name and asked him if he actually spoke the language of the court. The backing of mentors, family, and colleagues allowed him to stand down the judge's comment and instead cement his commitment to refining his practice and building up the network that serves him today. He, too, has likely never worked with an older attorney of Hispanic origin, but it has not stopped him from forming important mentorship relationships with others.

I have come to realize that while I may not soon find a fierce Latina attorney[212] to work for and emulate, an essential element of mentorship for me is accepting that not all mentors have to look like me. Around the time I made this realization, I started cultivating a mentorship relationship with Tom, a White attorney, who demonstrated many of the values I hold dear. A devoted husband and father, as a team leader he prefers to listen before interrupting or deciding. He has a deep desire to understand the world around him and is a voracious reader of books on politics, economics, history, and leadership. Every time we have lunch, I leave with a notepad full of book and podcast recommendations. I was first impressed by the intelligence of his questions and his desire to understand the systems that applied to his team's work.

I proposed lunch at a local pizza place to discuss mentorship, a topic about which he was enthusiastic. He recounted the story of a powerful mentor of his. He had been a young lawyer working in a law firm that had attracted the talents of a former politician, a veritable living legend in his country. In the halls, colleagues passing the office of this icon would stand straighter and quieter. Tom happened to meet him in the course of an assignment and was immediately impressed by the icon's intelligence, worldliness, and grace. On business lunches with clients, Tom's mentor would invite him to come along to absorb and learn. "I was basically carrying his suitcase, but it was an opportunity to watch him in action that was invaluable to me," said Tom.

Tom's eyes smiled when he told the story of going with his mentor to an Italian restaurant that floored him. His mentor was everything a lawyer should be and seemed to exude wit and sophistication. Coming from a middle-class family with no attorneys in the immediate family, Tom was uninitiated in this new world and could not wait to invite his brilliant wife (an attorney herself) to dine at the restaurant as well.

When he later went on to a position within a challenging ministry, his ability to meet professional challenges but also cultivate meaningful relationships with key individuals, including another iconic mentor, would polish him into a service-oriented leader in his own right. As I sat across from him and a dish full of spiced oil and spinach pizza, I appreciated I had a mentoring presence in front of me.

He was not a Latina, but he was sensitive to issues of race, having grown up in a country with significant historical struggles among racial lines. He was an attorney who dedicated himself to policy, governance, and social issues. He was a beloved husband whose eyes glistened with admiration as he spoke of his brilliant wife who had taken the courageous step to stay at home with their daughter. We invited them over for a night of Swiss fondue with meringues for dessert. The love they had for each other was evident as they smiled graciously, their teenage daughter indulging my own smaller children in games and conversation.

Perhaps Tom could not show me how to be navigate being a light-skinned Latina lawyer in Europe, but he (and his witty and gracious wife) could support and encourage me for a brief but critical moment in my career. I spent lunches with them telling bad jokes and listening to their stories as if the table were a campfire and their twinkling smiles were a silent and ever-tolerant smoky sky. Over many a business lunch over a handful of months, their conversation opened my eyes to the mentoring relationships and energy of people around me and taught me how to accept the guidance and support of others.

I now see the opportunity for mentorship not only in particular relationships but in powerful moments that I can string together as mottled and flickering lights illuminating my path. I see the stabilizing force of my peers who stand by my side, relacing their shoes and flexing before the whistle, as well as the energizing momentum of older mentors who warm the bleachers with their cries of audacious faith in my race.

Mentorship does not have to fit a particular paradigm; it just has to be meaningful for you. There is strength in representation and identification, as we have seen with the examples of former American President Barack Obama and US Supreme Court Justice Sonia Sotomayor. There is also power in seeking mentoring relationships around us, from those on the path of leadership, especially for people of color and women. Recently, I asked Ilaria about her former boss, and she replied that it had been years since they had connected. Distance and time changed the mentorship, but the power of that professional guidance is still felt by Ilaria, with fondness. Our mentorship needs change, and so do the relationships that fulfill them. Ultimately, seeking a mentor who can help you cope with challenges you are facing now is your next key action point—along with, quite simply, not giving up.

So, do not give up. Continue to walk the path of the (wo)man you wish to become, and you will begin to fill the shoes of your own ideal mentor.

CHAPTER TEN: REV YOUR ENTREPRENEURIAL ENGINE AND TAKE TO THE ROAD

> *I am a woman who came from the cotton fields of the South. From there I was promoted to the washtub [and then] the cook kitchen. And from there I promoted myself into the business of manufacturing hair goods and preparations[.] I have built my own factory on my own ground.*
>
> —MADAM C. J. WALKER[213]

They say you can find no better boss than yourself. Toiling with your own two hands to put bread on your table, you work harder and longer knowing you are investing and reinvesting in what is truly yours—the failures and the successes. Proving that necessity is the mother of invention, your mind moves with agility and ingenuity to solve problems in ways you never considered. The business grows proportionately to your investment and labor, and it can sometimes feel like your only limit is the sky. In some ways, this sounds idyllic or simplistic, but the fact of the matter is that entrepreneurs have that something, and we want it. How much happier would we be if we could just inject a sense of that muscle and motivation into our desk jobs? Creating meaningful professional relationships like mentorships and work spouses as we discussed in the previous chapters is only part of the puzzle. We need to feel invested in and accountable for our work to be fully engaged. If this speaks to you, nurturing an entrepreneurial attitude at work will be a frontline tactic to revitalizing your work life and boosting your career.

Evincing a cultivated elegance and rugged ease, Sébastien is as comfortable discussing high-end camera features as he is discussing fishing tackle. A few years ago, he jumped ship to manage an American luxury goods store in time for a campaign of innovation by a new CEO that has sent waves through their design department, e-commerce presence, and company culture. As we discussed in Chapter 3: Refocusing the Lens after Disappointment, the company culture of cultivating entrepreneurial attitudes has positively impacted his teams as well as his bottom line: "I am empowered in my store to treat it like my own enterprise—to take the short-term risks I believe will bring us long-term gain," said Sébastien.

The shift from a hierarchical management style toward Sébastien's person-driven, entrepreneurial leadership style was dramatic. Previously, customers were greeted by staff members who stood at attention beside sterile displays like stern gargoyles. Now, even casual customers feel welcomed by inviting smiles and creative display cases. It has been a subtle but forceful shift that has led Sébastien and his team to win regional sales awards for their innovation and results.

Part of the team that originally opened the store, Sébastien's colleague, Ju, is an exceptionally warm and patient sales associate. She continually works to create a safe space where one feels welcome, regardless of the price point of his or her purchases. At store events, the line of loyal customers that would form waiting for her attention served as a testament to her grace and professionalism. Under Sébastien's management, she has taken a step forward with bold and lucrative ideas for customer events and displays while also serving as a source of institutional knowledge and coaching for the newcomers to her team. In an industry where men dominate management positions, the mentorship Ju receives is precious and a direct reflection of the support Sébastien himself has received. She herself is too humble to admit it, but Ju exudes leadership potential that attracts clients as well as colleagues—a quality that her manager, Sébastien, visibly encourages in his team. To make good on this, he tries to see each person on his team at least once a day, saying:

> *When I don't, I lose the opportunity to do two things. One is to personally encourage each team member—to let them feel seen and appreciated. And, the second is the opportunity to reinforce my leadership style. I want my team to feel empowered not only under the brand, but as members of my team. You are not just working for [a well-respected and beloved centuries-old brand], you are working for me.*

The sense of ownership and empowerment encouraged by Sébastien's corporate office has been touted by management gurus like Simon Sinek[214] and institutions like *Harvard*

Business Review,[215] *Business Insider*,[216] and *Forbes*.[217] Having an entrepreneurial spirit in leading a business means tapping into an entrepreneur's passion and then solving problems as if they were sheerly ours. When a company neglects to foster entrepreneurship, it risks not only losing exceptional talent but even making competition for itself. A close example is Latino businessman Alonso, who left his job as foreman in his mid-thirties to open his own construction business after being turned down for a modest raise. Less than half a decade later, he has grown his business into a success story despite the economic pressures that closed down or threatened many of his competitors, including his old boss who likely saw Alonso's language, business, and personal skills as threats.

Instead of building a partnership and fighting to keep Alonso, Alonso's former employer lost Alonso's formidable skills and business acumen as a linguistic and cultural bridge between predominantly Anglo-American, English-speaking general contractors and Latino Spanish-speaking day laborers. After calculating how many contracts a month he would need to feed his small family, Alonso left his narrow-minded employer. Using only his own contacts and staying clear of his former boss' turf (not so much out of respect as out of adherence to his own high moral code), Alonso quickly went about the work of building his business. He put his workers first. He made sure they were taken care of in terms of health and well-being. He also personally trained them to ensure they understood what level of quality he expected from them. On pay days, he could be found in front of his driveway sharing plates of his wife Grace's exceptional cooking and cold beers from his garage fridge (the same Grace from Chapter 2: Discrimination Focus on the Motherhood Penalty and Fatherhood Bonus Dichotomy).

If the health of a tree can be seen in its fruit, then it is no surprise that Alonso and Grace have helped set up many former employees in their own business ventures. They have become not only small business owners but community leaders whose passion, imagination, and pragmatism continue to inspire everyone around them. Alonso says that "there are two types of people in this world: employers and employees." I think that is true regardless of whether you are self-employed or under contract to someone else. That being said, while the mentality of an employer—of an entrepreneur—can be found in an "employee," hiring managers (and would-be entrepreneurs) should note that not every entrepreneur makes a great addition to a staff.

There are entrepreneurs, and there is entrepreneurial spirit. Confusing the two can result in lost wages, time, and talent for employers, hiring managers, and candidates themselves.[218] Pure entrepreneurs will tend to divert their creativity and energy toward their passion projects until they are ready to fly off on their own, whereas employees with an entrepreneurial spirit will thrive on contributing to a larger business and revel in the day-to-day functioning of their employer. For the latter, encouraging independence and influence results in new, interesting proposals and approaches. Mere financial rewards will not be enough, so smart employers and managers will need to ensure the requisite time and space required for the kind of innovation that is at the heart of entrepreneurial drive. A head of research and innovation who oversaw his former company tripling its patent filing before striking out on his own, David says that "failure is a key ingredient to innovation" and, therefore, for the entrepreneurial spirit. No promising entrepreneur can be afraid of failure; she understands it is integral to her learning.

The other thing entrepreneurs know in addition to being unafraid of failure is trusting their guts. Funnily, it turns out that all that "gut-trusting" is rooted in more than just handed-down wisdom. Author of *Focus: The Hidden Driver of Excellence*,[219] Daniel Goleman talks about the connection between the prefrontal area of the brain (the part that focuses on the present) and the midbrain, in particular the amygdala (the part that focuses on emotions and dangers).[220] He tells a story[221] from the annals of neurology about a corporate attorney named "Elliot." Elliot had surgery to remove a prefrontal brain tumor that appeared at first to be a success. Elliot continued to score highly on intelligence tests and maintained his attention and memory, but the attorney could no longer hold down a job. By the time Elliot went to renowned neurologist Dr. Antonio Damasio,[222] he had been divorced and was living with his brother. After examining Elliot, Dr. Damasio was befuddled. There seemed to be nothing wrong with him until Dr. Damasio asked Elliot when they could see each other again. Despite Elliot's ability to explain the rationale for choosing various appointment times, he could not make the simple decision of choosing one. The surgery had removed the orbitofrontal cortex, which connects the frontal lobes to emotional centers in the brain. It was there that experience resided—a kind of memory database base rife with connections to the gut. Dr. Damasio had discovered the importance of the connection between the logical and emotional centers in the brain and their fundamental roles in decision-making.[223] He called them somatic markers. Elliot had lost the ability to tune into his body, his "gut," and with that, had lost his ability to make even simple decisions.

Linking back to entrepreneurial spirit, it is telling that Goleman also notes that founders tend to say the same thing: "I am a voracious gatherer of information but if it does not 'feel' right, I will not go along with the deal." Goleman says this aligns with the somatic marker hypothesis:

> *Essentially, [Damasio] reasons, when you're thinking about a course of action, you imagine your body to be in the potential situation, and you get, in layman's terms, a 'good' or 'bad' feeling about it. It's not that right decisions come from that sort of feeling alone, but, Damasio argues, those 'somatic markers' filter away lots of alternatives; they're a shortcut to decision-making.[224]*

In addition to a strong sense of ownership and trusting one's gut, entrepreneurship is characterized by the hunger for achievement. At its most basic level, an entrepreneurial mindset is about knowing what you want and making it happen. Sounds so easy, right? If you are like many of us, the hardest part is knowing what you actually want. How do you want to spend your minutes, talent, resources? When you close your eyes to imagine it, do you only see the many ways you could fail, or can you dare to see the many ways you could succeed? Author of *Start with Why*[225] and *Leaders Eat Last*,[226] Simon Sinek says that non-entrepreneurs will only see the obstacles along the path. In contrast, entrepreneurs lead the way, and as leaders, they often have followers. Managers, on the other hand, may have authority over their employees, but without leadership, they neither inspire nor guide. Inversely, there are leaders who are non-authorities but who absolutely guide, motivate, protect, and persuade others who willingly choose to "follow" them.

Those kinds of natural leaders can be found everywhere in a company. It is the trusted colleague in HR who is sought out for the compassionate but neutral way she manages conflict. It is the project manager whose advice on finding a way forward is in such high demand that she must occasionally escape home to get some work done. It is the lawyer with a line out the door of people waiting for the crafting of a precisely worded email, and it is the low-profile IT manager who day in and day out shows up for each of his teammates.

To think like an entrepreneur and inspire like a leader, Sinek says you have to understand the "Golden Circle."[227] It is a simple idea, but he says it separates the companies we love from their cheap imitators: "every organization on the planet knows what they do," and some even know "how" they do it; but only a few companies understand "why" they do what they do. In his view, the "why" is at the heart of the matter. It was the driving force of the entrepreneur who built a multimillion-dollar company in just a handful of years or a coffee shop that saw thriving sales within its first year of opening. Coming from a marketing background, Sinek finds Apple's messaging particularly compelling: "If Apple were like everyone else, a marketing message from them might sound like this: 'We make great computers. They're beautifully designed, simple to use and user friendly. Want to buy one?'"[228] Instead, at the core of all of Apple's marketing message is an inverse of this thinking—placing the "why" at the forefront:

> [In e]verything we do, we believe in challenging the status quo. We believe in thinking differently. The way we challenge the status quo is by making our products beautifully designed, simple to use and user friendly. We just happen to make great

computers. Want to buy one?[229]

Because entrepreneurs or founders often embody their companies' respective "whys," when they go, they can leave a rudderless ship if they fail to inject their sense of purpose into the company DNA. Founders facing the challenge of sharing their entrepreneurial mindset with their teams can make the difference of sink or swim for their companies, but what about those of us sitting at our desks, feeling detached from company ethos and powerless to affect it?

To answer that question, I turned to a seasoned director at a well-known international organization. Jill was happy to meet and suggested a pizza lunch at a spot near the United Nations Geneva Headquarters. Bearing that rare combination of actual humility and authority, Jill has spent decades in management and has seen many people come and go. When I asked her what she would recommend to someone who felt uninspired by their workplace and wanted to cultivate an entrepreneurial spirit, she responded with an example. She recalled a young woman on her team, "a high potential" who had left the team after being denied a request for a promotion. Knowing the teammate wanted more but fearing the teammate would feel called out during the conversation, Jill did not bring the issue out in the open. Saying this with regret on her face, she spoke of how she wished she had been able to help the high potential concentrate on her sphere of influence and find motivation in vertical growth and training while planning for concrete milestones to work toward. Neither said anything until it was too late, and Jill always wondered what would have happened if she had been able to reach her in time. It can be exceptionally difficult to focus on our potential when we are living in the shadow of others' perceptions or a misguided sense that we are not allowed to reach our dreams, Jill said.

Inevitably, adopting an entrepreneurial mindset to combat dejection or demotivation must start with the resolution of our basic dilemma: What do we want and what will we do to get it? Part of that equation includes conversations—with our bosses, our colleagues, our loves ones, or at least ourselves.

A seasoned trade lawyer related a similar story to me. Rico had felt like he had reached a glass ceiling when it came to his career development, but he could not contemplate leaving his job. So, he started working on blogs and podcasts and other side projects. He concentrated on the sphere of influence he could expand and refused to live in the shadow of the promotion he could not have. He started feeling more content in the office and volunteering for opportunities he was previously pessimistic about. He found himself taking on more and more responsibility, filling his time with his passion projects and new assignments in the office.

Like Rico, I had a lull in my career development before a significant change of company leadership. Realizing I could not directly affect the shifting company direction, I decided I would focus on what I had, not what I lacked. I would work on expanding my sphere of influence. Though not naming it as such, I wanted to take an entrepreneurial approach. I started focusing on listening to my clients and being fully present for them. I focused on my service to them, not just the dopamine-soaked satisfaction of offering the "right" answer. Not realizing it, I was preparing myself for a significant career step. My projects and work relationships took on new meaning and provided me immense satisfaction. I sought out mentorship opportunities and cultivated a more strategic perspective of my own work and role in my company. It was this bottom-up strategy that changed the path of my career irrevocably, but what happens when having an entrepreneurial spirit means getting constantly crushed?

An HR professional, Lily had been caught in the crosshairs of a management tug-of-war that was no longer tolerable, so she took her severance package and went off to write up a business proposal. Over burgers and pints, she told me that her path toward her own consulting firm went on a short detour when she was recruited to head a large group's branch offices. Later, when a restructuring had her looking back at the business proposal, like many women dissatisfied with the corporate ladder, Lily decided to go into consulting. Lily has been hustling for almost three years with no sign of stopping. She joins more and more women, according to Sarah Horowitz, founder and director of the Freelancers Union in New York, whose

> *lives play out in stages that don't fit well with a corporate world dominated by men. By our thirties, many women are starting families and struggling with taking time away from the office. By our forties, we're often hitting the glass ceiling in terms of pay and promotions. By our fifties and sixties, unfortunately, we're often being ignored altogether.* [230]

Referencing a 2015 study of freelancers in the United States, Horowitz says that freelancers are not monolithic, in particular for part-time work. Some are retirees who want to keep themselves busy, some are women who chafe under a rigid forty-hour work week and a demanding family schedule, and others are "moonlighters" who take side gigs for the extra money.[231] Interestingly, a 2014 study[232] of almost two thousand freelancers found that 53% were women, most of whom reported needing the income to supplement their inadequate salaries.

For others, pursuing a side gig is a financially responsible way of opening a new business. Larry was working as an attorney when he decided to open a small tech-based consulting business. He had just married his high school sweetheart and had a little one on the way. He did not feel comfortable giving up the security of a partnership-track position in a well-established law firm. It took him a couple of years, including time spent on research and development, but by the time he was ready to discuss his business with his partners, he had a solid customer base and an attractive business that allowed him to pursue an interest in fields totally disconnected to the practice of law. It has done very well, enabling him to hire employees and rent an office. In the meantime, he has maintained his main job as a major source of stability for his family.

Entrepreneurs boast greater physical and mental well-being[233] despite often taking a hit financially, especially in the early years; but leaving a salaried job to start a passion project or even just picking up a side gig might not be the right answer for you. Maybe you are still waiting for that one great idea or just want the spark back. The key may be a heightened sense of autonomy, which brings us back to capturing that sense of entrepreneurship in the office. Recognizing autonomy as a key driver for your motivation can be very important. One of Cara's most driven moments on a professional level involved the development of a complex compliance program. It required that she contact various relevant departments across her company and make champions of her colleagues. Even when she was picking up the slack in other areas, she was motivated and fully tuned in. She was designing and building a program based on the cooperation and input of many, founded on her own research and risk-assessment. Just like Simon Sinek says of entrepreneurs, she had identified what she wanted and did what she needed to do to achieve it. Her spark had returned. She recognized it anew in her entrepreneurial colleagues, including Séamus, a senior policy expert who relished his job managing industry stakeholders. He enjoys cultivating an autonomy that many of his peers lack—partly because of certain technical niceties but also because he fiercely guards his independence behind disarming transparency and competence.

He runs his team like an enterprise and protects his teammates. Despite being a fascinating orator, he challenges his reports to take on presentations and speaking engagements so that they can blossom. They admit turning down promotions and external job offers just to stay with him. He takes on policy risks with eyes wide open—unapologetically seeking counsel from trusted industry and technical giants. His roots in his community are deep, and he has a story for every occasion. But he has maintained a certain humility that allows him to learn and listen. Despite rampant change and toxic waves of infighting, he has steadfastly held on—creating an island of security and productivity that continues to lead the discussion. When asked if he would lay off someone for performance issues without warning, he replies, "No, barring certain extreme circumstances." His team has become itself a part of his business, like a mom and pop shop that stands out in the neighborhood.

Ultimately, having a true entrepreneurial mindset means more than just accountability, autonomy, and leadership. It means growth or, as Richard Branson, cofounder of a multinational venture capital conglomerate, puts it, "being willing to learn, being happy to make mistakes, being eager to experiment."[234] He continues:

All too often, talented people have fixed mindsets and are unwilling or unable to make the necessary changes to improve. When that happens, ideas stagnate, businesses stop growing, people stop learning.

An attitude like this puts agency squarely back into our laps: What is our sphere of influence? Who do we trust, and who trusts us back? What is our skillset? Where is our company going, and can we line up with that?

Having an entrepreneurial mindset does not have to mean quitting our day jobs to start a dog walking business. Instead, think of it as a challenge, an exercise in removing yourself from situations that frustrate you or having the guts and ingenuity to change them. If your work were a problem to be solved, without the triggering emotions of rejection, shame, or inadequacy, could you devise a new angle of attack that would give you different results? How would your entrepreneurial hero do it? And when you are the boss, ask yourself what you can do to trust your team more, letting them try their path through trial and error to find success. With an entrepreneurial tweak to your lens, your main concern will fall into focus, and it is then up to you to decide how much of yourself you will put into making your dreams come true at your desk job—no matter how big you may let those dream be.

SECTION 4: FISH OR CUT BAIT! DECIDING TO LEAVE, STAY, LEAD, OR PRAY

CHAPTER ELEVEN: YOU KNOW IT NOW. I KNEW IT THEN. IT'S TIME TO GO.

Two roads diverged in a yellow wood,
And sorry I could not travel both
And be one traveler, long I stood
And looked down one as far as I could
To where it bent in the undergrowth;
Then took the other, as just as fair,
[...]
[and] doubted if I should ever come back.

—ROBERT FROST[235]

Olivia stepped out of the meeting room, her heart beating in her ears. A mix of frustration and exhaustion filled her chest as one hot tear escaped. She walked quickly, with her laptop under her arm and her eyes fixed on the floor. Reaching her desk, she sank back into her leatherback chair. The meeting replayed in her mind like a silent film. As if pointing to an imaginary theater screen, she thought, "Right there I should have said 'I quit.'" But she did not and instead added another miserable day to her pile, like many of us have. In the throes of workplace frustration, daydreaming about quitting can become an irresistible escape. We read articles about the changing job market and then email a colleague a punchy story about some audacious Wallstreet-type who blasted his execs a scathing farewell. It relieves the pressure for a moment, but sometimes, these fantasies become stepping-stones to a permanent departure. Sometimes, the best way to move forward is to stop.

Sitting in my home office with a silly, half-empty *world's greatest lawyer* coffee mug, I can imagine telling you, dear reader, the story of how I quit a job that in many ways I loved, with a calm confidence in my retelling of it that might make you think my decision was inevitable and obvious. The clarity of hindsight can do that to a story, but the truth is it took a few years. Maybe you too dream of taking a path less traveled, so you might understand how I looked longingly through bookstore windows or lingered at coffee breaks discussing workplace studies and theories. Maybe like you, I would then neglect this small, wild fantasy as I chased my older, vocational passion through new projects and productive collaborations. As I began to know my colleagues better, my contributions to their work deepened my investment in their success, and in turn, theirs in mine. But the years were rolling by and another decennial birthday loomed; the "now" part of "now or never" was becoming more and more salient.

Another autumn had started chilling the air when I found myself confronting that "now." My work felt reactionary and circular—the brambles and twists in my path yearned to be pruned and lit, yet there were no shears nor flashlight. In a place of indecision, I had to cut a new path for myself and quit expecting someone else to do it for me. To paraphrase a beloved mentor named Bill from the American South, "That dog won't hunt—only a fool expects a house dog to lead the pack." How many of us repeat our daily grind blindly hoping our same actions will yield different results, that others will change for us, or that we ourselves will just wake up one mythical morning magically having become the hero we have been waiting for.

I had the workings for a book, and maybe I could freelance on the side. I consulted several close friends, sympathetic mentors, and my family over long phone calls and three-hour Saturday morning coffees. Miles away, my sister said into the phone, "You can do this. I believe in you." I spoke rationally about my household budget and local unemployment statistics and, like a good student, presented the risks and probability of possible consequences—to which my husband said simply and compassionately, "I believe in you. We can do this."

I called up Robert, the no-nonsense diplomat, to tell him of my plan. He listened until I ran out of things to say. Without judgment on his face, he asked calmly, "I hear you, and if you must go, then you must. But is there any way in which you could stay?" I let the question sit with me, went home to make a list of options, and consulted colleagues and professional contacts on whether any of these options could work. I also asked myself whether I could further lean on my network, my work friends, my mentors. Could I boost my entrepreneurial spirit or simply change my perspective? No, I had already tried all these, adding preceding years that in many ways I was deeply grateful for but that did not resolve the underlying problem. I wanted to build, and I had run out of room. I wanted not only more for my career but more for my life. Having lost my father in my teen years, I have often asked myself during pivotal decisions a morbidly sharp but simple question: What will matter to me on my deathbed? Will I remember this fear and regret betting on a dream, or will I seethe with pity for myself, having never risked anything for myself at all?

The days leading up to my quitting were not easy. Night after night, I dreamed about being chased by zombies as my fear of the unknown, regardless of all my calculations and support, threatened to bury my nerve. In the middle of a particularly fitful night, I drafted a resignation letter on my phone's notepad. It was short and sweet and made me smile with genuine gratitude, but I still could not sleep. I avoided social contact. Friends asked me what was wrong, and awkward ad hoc attempts were made to check on me. The days had felt like months and the hours like days, but a sense of peace as well as sadness came over me as I printed out my resignation letter.

I came to work early, calmed myself with a hot cup of black coffee, and quietly looked out onto the street outside the office windows. There is, of course, no telling the kinds of reactions you might receive once you take the leap. Some are happy or even proud to see you leave for higher ground; you can expect shock, consternation, sadness, and even anger. I organized my goodbyes as gently as I could and relished the reminiscing over lunches and coffee breaks.

For some, the best way to take a break from work for a short-term project is to take a sabbatical, but sabbaticals are tricky things, just like a change of title, scope, reporting line, or salary, to entice someone to stay. More often than not, these tactics, if they do not address the underlying reason an employee wishes to leave, will only prolong the inevitable departure.[236] Will you face resentments and distance when you return from sabbatical, receive a pay bump, or change reporting lines? Whatever counteroffer you receive may taste like bitter desserts when it comes wrapped in unspoken questions of "Happy now? Can we trust you to stay?" or "If they think you're worth that now, why weren't they paying you that earlier?"[237]

Good reasons to quit are varied,[238] like finding a new job or new place to live, loathing your job or the toxic environment, wanting to go back to school or change careers, becoming ill, experiencing a significant lifestyle change, or simply knowing in your "gut" that it is time to go.

There is no crystal ball that will guarantee your life will be better after a decision to quit. That being said, it is important to trust the connection between our reptilian brains and our "guts,"[239] so to speak.[240] According to Emeran A. Mayer,[241] "The concept that the gut and the brain are closely connected, and that this interaction plays an important part not only in gastrointestinal function but also in certain feeling states and in intuitive decision making, is deeply rooted in our language." The complex, bidirectional system within the "gut-brain crosstalk" can both positively and negatively affect gastrointestinal health and eating disorders, as well as affecting motive, intuition, and other high cognitive functions.

I asked a young manager, Olivia, how long it took her to decide it was time to resign. She said that she knew in twenty-seven minutes. She had been struggling with a lack of managerial support and direction for a couple of years, from the moment her former boss was promoted to another department several buildings away. Even though she could still lean on her former boss during uplifting lunches, the absence of the previous support and the increased expectations from her new boss created a vicious feedback loop of need and demand that ultimately broke—almost anticlimactically—after yet another unanswered request for support. Depending on your perspective, her decision took either minutes or months. In any case, that inner "voice" had grown too loud to ignore.

I asked Olivia whether there had been any attempts to retain her talent, given that she was widely respected and appreciated in her company. She replied, "Not at all. My HR Manager said she was not surprised since I had expressed the desire to quit the year before. Then two other managers tried to convince me to join their teams, but it was too late for me." The dream for her future had been growing like mushrooms in a neglected garden. She was unapologetic, with little time for indecision, misplaced concern, and discriminatory, mean-spirited comments intended to intimidate. Olivia's departure threw her team for a loop. It would cost thousands and be months before she was replaced. It made me realize how critical talent retention strategies can be to the long-term health of a company. It is not a nice-to-have or an exercise in copying and pasting another company's policy from the internet. A good retention policy has to reflect the company's values as well as support an empathic and people-oriented direction. According to recruitment agency Robert Half:

> *Succeeding in your employee retention efforts requires you to think about things from the team's point of view. All employees are different, of course, and each has unique desires and goals. But it's a safe bet to assume that all of them want to know they are being paid at or above market rates and have good benefits. They want to feel that they are appreciated by their employer and treated fairly. They want to be challenged and excited by the job they're asked to do. An effective employee retention program addresses all of these concerns. But it also goes beyond the basics.[242]*

According to the US Department of Labor Statistics, there were about 7.3 million jobs open in June of 2019[243]. During that same time, 5.7 million people were hired and 5.5 million left their jobs (voluntarily and involuntarily). Of the separations, the quitting rate remained stable at 2.3% and the termination rate clocked in at 1.1%. The remaining separations were due to retirement, death, disability, and transfers to other locations of the same firm. Not surprisingly, turnover rates were highest in retail and hospitality jobs and lowest in government jobs for the (non-farm) sectors analyzed.

Comparatively, in Switzerland in 2017,[244] 19.3% of people exercising a professional activity left their jobs (voluntarily or involuntarily) within a year. Of the overall 12.7% separation rate, a full 6.6% either quit or were fired. Global voluntary turnover rates in 2016 were 9.6%, and in Europe they were 7.1%.[245]

Replacing employees who leave can cost an organization as much as 33%[246] of an employee's annual compensation package, including both wages and benefits. Moreover, companies with high turnover rates risk being outperformed by other firms by as much as four times.

For the owner of a local beer shop from Chapter 8: Behind Every Great (Wo)man Is a Great Work Spouse, the decision to quit had been in the making for several months. As a successful businessman, he had laid out a plan to allow him to slowly leave his former position while he followed his dream of founding his own brick-and-mortar establishment. He partnered up with a beer connoisseur, combining the quirkiness of their contrasting personalities and complementary skills to build a popular spot at a time when there were few craft beer shops in the community. He kept working part-time in his old job while setting up his business. For him, it worked swimmingly. It allowed him to collect a paycheck while he invested everything else in launching his business. By the time he was ready to fully quit, his business was thriving, and he had a handful of employees and a steady stream of loyal customers.

Regardless of its context, quitting can be frightening. According to one employment poll in the United Kingdom, workers consider quitting at least sixteen times a year![247] But that does not mean they act on it. According to the same poll, Londoners change jobs only every seven years on average, one year later than the average of British workers overall. That being said, most reported considering a career change as much as ten times a year, and one-third reported having been retrained already in the past. Many also believed that a career change after forty-seven was unwise. In Switzerland, conventional wisdom dictates that career changes after fifty are very difficult, if not impossible.

Still, in the US, statistics suggest that the average worker will change careers at least seven times during a lifetime.[248] The trend toward changing jobs or careers is only increasing. As echoed by one technical expert I spoke with, who recently went on maternity leave, "I'm just sick of looking for a new job every two years. The job market just isn't what it used to be for our parents." She is not wrong in intimating that the job market has changed in recent decades. The average lengths of stay in one job considerably shortened in the US from 2014 to 2016,[249] e.g., 4.5 years to 4 years for women and 4.2 overall, remaining unchanged in 2018.[250]

Preparing for the aftermath of quitting is different for everyone, but there are certain similarities. Zoe Weiner, writing "9 Things to Do after You Quit Your Job from Someone Who

Just Did It"[251] for *Bustle* says, "There are typical answers to that question, like 'stay on good terms with everyone' and 'make sure your finances are in order,' but what can you do during your time off for you?" Recognizing possible downtime can be scary, but she nevertheless emphasizes that the first order of business is just to breathe.

Quitting is an emotional business, and processing feelings of sadness and loss as much as anger and relief can take effort and time. Depending on the reasons why leaving was necessary, Weiner suggests taking the time to enjoy the free time to read trashy novels or sleep for half-days or take up crocheting or watch long loops of YouTube videos; or taking a seventeen-week solo tour to Copenhagen, South Africa, Namibia, Botswana, Zambia, Malawi, Tanzania, Kenya, Australia, New Zealand, and Japan.

Making a plan and deciding when and for what kind of jobs you will apply can be essential to avoiding slipping into a self-loathing cycle of sleep, take-out, TV, and rewearing dirty laundry. It is also an opportunity to visit cultural sites, read, meet up with not only friends but also with inspiring figures from the community, start hobbies, and find associations for various activities. Donating time to a charity can give structure and purpose to the day, as can writing a book or creating an online platform for friends and family to feel connected to your musings. It may not be often that one has time off, so considering that time as precious can plants seeds of future callings in the fertile space of all those newly emptied days.

On my last day, I packed up my books and papers into a couple of bags. I had already said goodbye to many, but I nevertheless felt the pang of loss as I gave hugs and handshakes, handed over my laptop and phone, and walked out into the crisp gray afternoon. In the inescapable neighborhood of our inner dialogues, questions have a habit of congregating at the corner of *end* and *beginning*.

When I left my job to have my first child, I questioned my identity. Did I still want to make a living with my degree? I casually toyed with writing but did not manage to get more than a few scenes of fiction onto a page. I wondered if staying at home would be a viable option, but I quickly found anger in the furious solitude of my days. I gave birth four weeks after the end of my contract, and within seven weeks of that, I had dusted off my resume to apply for a job that a former colleague had forwarded me. It was the first and only job I had applied to since university almost half a decade before. I had answered my question; I resolutely missed working at a desk solving problems, earning my own money, and working in a team.

When I left my next job, the questions that greeted me were again about identity and the way in which I wanted to shape my future life. Could I complete a book? Would it mean anything to anyone? My husband suggested I put the questions on hold and take a proper two-week Christmas vacation like I had originally planned. We put up a fragrant tree and baked batch after batch of wintry delights. It felt like something was loosening in between breaking up grade-school quarrels and analyzing cartoon bad guy moves with my kids, decompressing over a smoky scotch with my husband on the sofa in front of an irreverent cooking show, inviting friends over for an organic French-born roast turkey *à l'Américaine* or Swiss fondue *moitié-moitié,* or just staring into our blinking Christmas tree.

By the time my new job as a writer started, I was champing at the bit for the relished structure and challenge of the office, so I got started on setting daily and weekly goals by which to measure my performance. I got into a habit of dressing for work and leaving home to write in a nearby coffee shop. I would order my coffee, tip generously, and get to work. My mornings were separated from the afternoons by a line of interviews and networking events. I kept my toes in the job search pool, took a course in starting businesses, and then did executive coaching. At the close of each workday, I would circle the wagons around word count graphs before extinguishing the computer screen that would relight the next morning.

During interviews with white-collar professionals from all fields, my questions turned more personal. Have you ever quit? Why would someone want to? How do level up in your career? What gets you up in the morning? Listening to unexpected twists in the career paths of my friends and former colleagues, I noticed that with growth also came pain and the chalky silence of waiting without certainty.

One such professional was Samta (from Chapter One: How Did I Get Here? Making Your Next Career Move), a public health professional in a family of four. Her career was going strong, but she and her partner needed more help with their twin infants. If her network in Europe and North America was already considerable because of her studies and research, in India her name opened doors. She figured it was time to take a calculated leap of faith, and they packed up their bags to live near her birth family. A few precious years passed, and as her girls reached school age, Samta knew it was time to move again and return to her husband's home.

Preparing to move across continents while looking for a new job, Samta pulled on strings to land a part-time job, figuring that once she had her kids set up in school, she would have tons of time to find something more permanent. Raising young children, however, took more energy than expected, and she easily got consumed by domestic projects. Pulling herself up by her bootstraps, Samta dug deeper, ringing up old school and work contacts. She landed her big break about a year or so later. Her one regret? Not having used that gap year to enjoy life more. She had been so caught up in the "them" and the "later" that she had spent precious little time on the "self" and the "now." Quitting might mean waiting and certainly means finding another source of income, but can quitting free up your energy and time to invest in yourself or others?

Unless you are quitting for another job, planning for what comes after is critical. How long can you afford to go without a paid job? Will there be a gap in your CV, and how will you address it? If you are going to look for a new job, what differences are you looking for? Knowing what to look for in a new employer can be more important than earning more money or having a better position.

Pulling the plug on a job can be daunting, especially if you do not know what comes (or what you want) next. Here is a simple exercise. Imagine yourself at the end of your life. You know all the answers to the questions you have about what will happen, and it fills with you a calming serenity. You feel warmly confident in your gentle wisdom, so now look back at this moment with the forgiving lens of hindsight.

Do you see something new? If your gentle future self could speak, what story would that warmly confident soul tell you now? Close your eyes.

Many of us will have imagined regret regardless of whether it was projected buyer's remorse or the pang of what could have been. Few of us might have seen the cascading roll of the incredible life we had after we quit (You know what you must do), but others are dreaming of the new life they want to let them stay. If that dream speaks to you, then this next chapter is for you.

CHAPTER TWELVE: DECIDING TO STAY AND PURSUE PERFECTION

> *You have to fall in love with your work. Never complain about your job. You must dedicate your life to mastering your skill. That's the secret of success...*
>
> —JIRO ONO[252]

A balding eighty-five-year-old Japanese man exudes a serene and focused power as he stands over his small ephemeral masterpiece.[253] As the camera pans from the glistening morsel of fish and rice back to his face, the expression in his eyes flickers between stern silence and querying interest. Jiro Ono says he has never hated his job a day in his long life. At eighty-two, he became the world's oldest three-star Michelin chef for his small sushi restaurant featuring a concerto of painstakingly perfected dishes. Though his tone is meditative, there are equal parts childish exhilaration and long-exercised control in his words: "I do the same thing over and over, improving bit by bit [...] trying to reach the top, but no one knows where the top is."[254]

For those of us who have decided to tie our careers to the shooting star of our ambition, deciding to stay in our jobs may be no less brave and no less difficult than deciding to leave. But as is often the case, if you thrive on challenges and innovation, the onus is on you to relight the campfires. American poet and essayist Ralph Waldo Emerson wrote, "To finish the moment, to find the journey's end in every step of the road, to live the greatest number of good hours, is wisdom."[255] So what if all it takes is just a different point of view?

Having spent his life in the restaurant business, Ono is driven by his belief in the practice of being a *shokunin* (craftsman or artisan in Japanese) that calls him to repeat each action of his craft with exacting daily care. It took him years to change the time octopus should be massaged (forty-five instead of thirty minutes) to ensure ultimate tenderness. In the documentary by David Gelb entitled *Jiro Dreams of Sushi*, an apprentice speaks about how it took him two hundred times making *tamagoyaki* (a Japanese omelet) before Jiro said it was of an acceptable quality. On the day his omelet was not thrown out, the apprentice recounts that he wept.

Of course, the general idea that practice makes perfect is nothing new. Malcolm Gladwell wrote about the ten thousand hours required to make a world-class expert in his book, *Outliers*.[256] He was seeking to understand the factors behind the making of truly exceptional and successful people. He looked at one 1990s study by psychologist K. Anders Ericsson at an elite academy of music in Berlin. The researchers had divided up groups of musicians into three: those with potential to become world class soloists, those who were proficient, and those who preferred to teach music in the public-school system. To their surprise, the researchers found that neither prodigal skill nor innate genius correlated with mastery. The biggest predictor of mastery was the amount of time spent in practice. The highest skilled musicians had all started studying music around five years old, gently increasing their weekly hours of practice until by the time they were about twenty, they were practicing some thirty hours a week. Each of these high-potential soloists had practiced an average of ten thousand hours by the time they were twenty. The second group? Some eight thousand hours. And the third group? About four thousand hours. It appeared their expertise was not as much a matter of some inherent or commonly unattainable gift as it was a result of their working harder than their equally gifted counterparts—"much, *much* harder."[257]

How does a normal human foment that kind of sustained passion? Browsing online shots of perfectly staged coffee cakes, crocheted beanies, or home-crafted beer can be seductive, but mastery is so much more than sheer appearances.[258] Whether we hear it or not, there is a waterfall of power in the passing drip of our hours.

Before I started writing, I kept a running note on my phone with topics and questions brought up during my cherished off-the-clock talks. The list became an outline, and the outline became an Excel spreadsheet sheet with daily word counts. The fear I felt in the gunmetal silence after quitting dissipated under the syncopated rhythm of my daily typing. A few thousand words in, I relaxed and started believing in each step I took on my path "of a thousand miles." I had realized that what I did with the hours of my days was what I was doing with my life.

We often fall victim to the cinematic fairy tales of finding ultimate satisfaction in big shiny moments or promotions. Spending hours in coffee shops with notes from interviews and a daily word count goal, I wondered: What if each step—executed exactly—is its own climax? Looking at the hours as their own end in the quiet mastering of our daily work, we can find inspiration from Jiro Ono's commitment to the tenets of being a *shokunin.*

Meeting my work wife for lunch, I shared my new outlook. As I put several hundred words on paper each day, I was not only writing for my fellow young urban professional feeling frustrated on his or her frenzied career path, but I was also fulfilling my own childhood dream of modestly penning my thoughts. Like a horde of ants crashing a picnic, our days can bring entire feasts to our mouths.

"Of course, that's the secret," Didi said. "Isn't it inspiring, though? We can do so much to determine the course of our lives. We have that privilege." Didi emphasized the word *privilege,* arching her eyebrows and lifting the corners of her mouth into a resting smile.

Staying at our desks in front of our blinking screens, we can exercise that privilege of using our hours to build a life of quiet mastery, even in modest domains. In the early 2000s, craftsmanship started taking on cachet in terms of marketing and tastes. With the hipster marketing trends, everything homemade, things made *à l'ancienne,* heritage vegetables, craft beers, and hand-dyed textiles came into vogue. A premium was placed on people, stores, and homes being expensively appointed in a way calculated to appear rural and rough-hewn. In *Esquire,* Richard Benson wrote:[259]

> *Anyone can see that craft's time has come. In Britain in 2015, you cannot move for people whose once-resolutely urban, style-conscious and modernist tastes have gone subtly country. They are visiting Soho Farmhouse, [...] listening to Mumford & Sons, [...] watching Grayson Perry reinvent pot throwing and tapestry, and/or reading James Rebanks's The*

Shepherd's Life, [and] drinking ale from a microbrewery (one opening every other day, while 20 pubs a week close).

Benson tracks the trend back to the mid-noughties with renewed preferences for single-speed bikes, rain boots and dated floral patterns as a response to the Iraq war. Then as soon as one trend installs itself among some, the backlash against it gains traction among others. Anti-hipsters mocked the dichotomy between spending hundreds on clothing and accessories to look essentially homeless or the race-to-the-bottom toward gimmicky über-hoppy, beer-producing microbreweries that put decades-old neighborhood pubs out of business. Regardless of which side you might have fallen on, the idealism of craftsmanship nevertheless came back to stay.

Given the average age of its acolytes, it is unsurprising then that the trend hit computer science circles where coding can be considered a repetitive task. A developer writes code to implement the function he or she so desires, like an artisan receiving a commission for a particular sculpture or piece of writing. In response to the "Agile Manifesto,"[260] with its emphasis on constant releases and iterations, the "Manifesto for Software Craftsmanship" goes one step further by also emphasizing the craft of writing "clean code."[261] It states:

As aspiring Software Craftsmen we are raising the bar of professional software development by practicing it and helping others learn the craft. Through this work we have come to value:

Not only working software,
   *but also **well-crafted software***

CHAPTER TWELVE: DECIDING TO STAY AND PURSUE PERFECTION | 169

Not only responding to change,
*but **also, steadily adding value**...*

Reminiscent of the ten years it takes to become a classically trained sushi chef, the manifesto has inspired some to entertain what it is to become a programmer in ten years[262]—to fly against the idea that five steps or twenty-four hours to a new talent is the most satisfying path to knowledge or accomplishment.

Like programmers, writers also craft products of sorts. For some authors, this has meant pursuing their craft for decades before producing great works. Describing the process of writing *Harry Potter and the Philosopher's Stone* as a single mother on government benefits, author J. K. Rowling said[263] that writing was the one thing in her life that she knew, beyond desperately loving her baby daughter; it was something she could and must do. From the age when she understood that books had to be written and did not merely spring from the ether, she wanted to write. So, she wrote compulsively through her late teens up to her twenties. And then one day on a train, she was struck by the idea of a boy, unaware that he was a wizard, going to a wizarding school. In 2017, *Forbes* named Rowling the highest-earning novelist worldwide and the third highest-paid celebrity.[264]

A craftsman does not need to be paid well or have celebrity to feel successful in the pursuit of perfecting his or her trade. I recently suggested the idea of craftmanship to two experienced professionals in high-performance fields. Jill replied, "But of course craftmanship exists. My father is a painter in his spare time, for example!" But what did that mean in white-collar work? Her partner, Emilie, towered over me with kind blue eyes and a tapered bob and muttered, "Mm-hmm. Well, that is what we do every day in customer service. We take pleasure in providing a service that may feel repetitive but brings real value to the customer. Perhaps it's just not thought of as a craft because there is nothing tangible, no product at the end of it."

Emilie is the stalwart kind of professional who expresses great pride in managing the details of her daily work. She dresses impeccably and takes painstaking care of her clients' needs and accounts. She sees herself as the first line of defense in the large multinational bank she works for, and she puts in long hours in the pursuit of doing things as they ought to be done. A humble and strong-willed woman, Emilie does not see herself as a master of any sorts, but when she received the promotion that she had been after for months, she celebrated wholeheartedly and whipped up a splashy homemade feast. In some ways, she reminds me of the Great Generation showing loyalty to their employers and trudging day in and day out, slowly building their dreams of homeownership and happy retirement that seemed eminently attainable with a bit of elbow grease and time.

Whether we are like Jiro perfecting a dish over decades, a hipster software developer adhering to a craftsman's code, a writer slugging through difficult pages line by line, or a customer-service representative making her clients' lives better one call at a time, there is room for mastery in the mundane regardless[265] of whether it takes more or less than ten thousand hours. But each hour is different depending on concentration and circumstance, and the interaction between the practice and the innate talent is an alchemy that is not easily explained (or copied).

Some professionals after a decade of niche work are stunningly brilliant, capable of contextualizing their specialty in a global context and reducing great complexity to digestible simplicity. Others have merely perfected their capacity to obey. They follow prefabricated processes they are incapable of innovating. True masters belong with the former, and while they are fundamentally the product of talent, drive, and often serendipity, they also require resilience. American professor and author Sarah Lewis writes:[266]

> *Mastery requires endurance. Mastery, a word we don't use often, is not the equivalent of what we might consider its cognate—perfectionism—an inhuman aim motivated by a concern with how others view us. Mastery is also not the same as success—an event-based victory based on a peak point, a punctuated moment in time. Mastery is not merely a commitment to a goal, but to a curved-line, constant pursuit.*

At its core, mastery is an enduring journey paved by moments of mindfulness. Can this mindfulness rekindle the flame of our hearth as we sit wide-eyed with frustration but also hope at our desks?

Over the last few decades, our collective attention spans have inarguably changed. It might still be trendy to value the homespun and handcrafted, but the notion of dedicating years (not just a few hours or weeks) to crocheting or handmaking sushi rolls is still rare. Author Daniel Goleman discussed the importance of attention in a compelling talk[267] in London. How often do we give our full attention, drop all our devices, and open up our posture when a colleague is talking? Not enough, but it is essential to efficient performance; the more an athlete concentrates now the better he or she does, now and next season.

Goleman also mentions the power of emotional distraction and that those accustomed to having their attention forcibly grabbed from one headline or app to another may never reach levels of mastery in anything if they are unable to master blocking out these distractions. Quite simply, flow is never reached. He defines *flow* as the height of attention while performing a task. For example, imagine world-class surgeons during hours-long surgeries or exquisitely tuned ballerinas in a ballet. Flow is not only necessary for great results, but it also feels good, like the oxytocin-flush you have when chatting up a work spouse over a gripping mug of morning coffee.

Inversely, letting the mind wander (the mirrored partner of focus) in between moments of flow is also required for robust creative processes. In mental free fall, Goleman says, we are able to make connections between remote elements in a creative way. At the office, we might kick ourselves for our moments of daydreaming or feel like grabbing a coffee to stare out the window is just a waste of time. But, in reality, allowing our brain a moment to wander between flashes of concentration is what enables us to be creative and innovative. It is an essential element of mindfulness as well as of craftsmanship.

Mindfulness feels like a buzzword these days, but it was actually popularized in the medical sector by Jon Kabat-Zinn in 1979. He had recruited chronically ill patients who were not responding well to their current treatment regimens for an eight-week stress-reduction pilot program. The successful pilot became a program called Mindfulness-Based Stress Reduction. According to Kabat-Zinn, mindfulness is "awareness that arises through paying attention, on purpose, in the present moment, non-judgmentally [...] in the service of self-understanding and wisdom."[268]

After his pilot, Kabat-Zinn went to a biotech startup and taught people how to engage in mindfulness. Kabat-Zinn lead a group of overstressed participants through mindfulness exercises for thirty minutes a day over eight weeks. Initially, the participants showed more activity in the right sides of their brain. After eight weeks, however, the brain activity started to tilt to the left, where some of the brain's more analytical functions operate. The participants were more fully engaged mentally in their work. Unsurprisingly, participants reported that they felt more satisfaction with their work.

Without a formal program like Kabat-Zinn's, mindfulness in the office is not an easy exercise, especially with the trends toward open floor plans that seem to be built to distract. It is no surprise, then, that top companies from Google to General Mills have started teaching mindfulness at work.[269] Since the ability to consciously go between focus and mind-wandering is pivotal for our ability to drive attention, learning mindfulness helps our brains learn to ignore workplace distractions, including emotion-ridden ones, that weaken our focus and cause us to become frustrated and waste time. Taking intentional meditative pauses and then bringing our attention back to our work can significantly strengthen our ability to focus, improving our satisfaction as well as our performance.

"The goal of mindfulness isn't to stop thinking, or to empty the mind. Rather, the point is to pay close attention to your physical sensations, thoughts, and emotions in order to see them more clearly, without making so many assumptions, or making up stories," writes David Gelles for the *New York Times*.[270]

One way to practice mindfulness is to exercise STOP:
- **S**top what you are doing
- **T**ake a deeep breath and focus on it.

- **O**bserve your body, your thoughts, and your surroundings.
- **P**roceed with your activity.

Go ahead and try it. Did you notice the sounds around you, the car whizzing by or your colleagues munching on their lunches or the spinning wheels of luggage being carted about? Try it at your next meeting or after a long chain of email for heightened focus and reduced stress.

The panacea of mindfulness is not just in improving attention and performance but also in its ability to reconfigure our brain activity, making more of us able to find pleasure and satisfaction in our daily tasks, regardless of how mundane they may be. When our attention is heightened and we are focused on the task at hand, we are in a better position to find neurological satisfaction in the flow of the moment.

With the exception of the few companies that have recognized the importance of mindfulness, the modern corporate world of ever-changing key performance indicators and management by objectives does little to foster the kind of mindfulness that could bring us mastery in the workplace. Instead, we can feel like cattle being herded toward the specter of the next big promotion that never comes or new challenges that are suspended, canceled, or indecorously handed to another. The exercise of mindfulness and the pursuit of mastery can feel like something undervalued.

Practicing a trade as old as disputes themselves, attorneys are familiar with the language of mastering one's craft when it comes to the practice of law. There is a notion that lawyers become better and their skillset more valuable as they age and gain experience, so much so that lawyers generally do not see the peak of their salary range until their fifties.[271] A hypothetical from my law school days illustrates this point. My Contracts professor, a grizzly and good-humored academic, asked us a tricky contractual dispute question. Goods had been promised; only some had arrived. There was a misunderstanding about pricing and half-typed up invoices, but no signed contract or order. Immediately, the students offered possible legal attacks and counterattacks. Astonished, the professor asked, "This is how you would advise your client? To fight? Propose that, and your client won't trust you anymore. He'll ignore you and pick up the phone to call his business partner to work it out. The medicine can't be worse than the disease." He offered wisdom born of experience: Just because you can pick up weapons does not mean you should.

Ultimately, the adamant professional who has learned his or her craft over thousands of mindful hours has much more to offer than a better service; they offer themselves the pleasure of flow and the satisfaction inherent in the practice of mastery. Change can be exciting, but mastery, flow, and mindfulness have their own siren's call capable of piercing the banality of our lives. Cultivating that perspective and recognizing the value of it can be an essential strategy for staying and thriving in a situation that could be otherwise frustrating. Considering that perfection is unattainable, you cannot fail at it, right? So, what you are afraid of in tilting your head toward the call?

CHAPTER THIRTEEN: WE WANT YOU! STAND UP AND LEAD.

> *When someone is cruel or acts like a bully, you don't stoop to their level. No, our motto is, when they go low, we go high.*
>
> —MICHELLE OBAMA[272]

Speaking at the Democratic National Convention in 2016, First Lady Michelle Obama gave an iconic speech, synthesizing her family's time in the White House and cementing herself as the unappointed leader that many around the world needed at a moment of social and rhetorical divisiveness. Asked about her words, Obama said:

> 'Going high' doesn't mean you don't feel the hurt, or you're not entitled to an emotion… It means that your response has to reflect the solution. It shouldn't come from a place of anger or vengefulness. Barack and I had to figure that out. Anger

may feel good in the moment, but it's not going to move the ball forward.[273]

Contemplating the calls for Obama herself to run for president, on an unremarkable Sunday morning of pancakes and laundry, I asked my husband a question I had been pondering for years: What makes a great leader? The First Lady was not an elected official but spoke with the kind of charismatic and authoritative leadership politicians dream of. Listening to her took me out of myself and made me want to become more than what I was. I contemplated what *going high when others went low* would look like in a life smaller than Obama's: maybe giving space (but not fuel) to a negative colleague, building something great even if another would take the credit, or giving someone with an unfortunate reputation a chance to improve. Perhaps in your life going high would mean something entirely different, but what connects us regardless of career path or ambition is the call to action. Going high "means that your response has to reflect the solution." Going high sounds like service-oriented acts of leadership, no matter how small or big, and for those of you for whom leaving or staying at your job is not the answer, standing up to lead may be your path to finding satisfaction in the workplace.

As leaders come in different shapes and sizes, so too do our notions of leadership evolve. Living at a time when our access to each other through media is unprecedented, we see multimillionaires[274] being made through online sales, gurus[275] with online channels viewed one hundred million times over, and millionaire YouTubers[276]. Perhaps it challenges our sense of leadership to say that a young YouTube star with hundreds of millions of followers is a leader, but leadership is talked about in as many ways as there are leaders themselves. One particularly compelling definition of leadership comes from thought-leader Simon Sinek. In his TED Talk from 2009 "How Great Leaders Inspire Action,"[277] Sinek breaks down leadership to its bare component: someone with followers. Great leaders do something more, however, than merely wield power or employ intimidation. Put in another way, leadership is something outside mere management. [278]

Leadership and management are, however, often confused. If you talk to a struggling manager about her team's expectations of her as a manager and refer to "leadership," you will not be surprised when you are met with utter bewilderment or, at best, an ironic complaint about service-oriented leadership being too rare. Just like leadership does not require institutional authority, management is merely administration without a sense of direction and mobilization. Confusing the two dooms our struggling manager to aspirations befitting a simple administrator. On the other hand, deepening our understanding of leadership can open us to the possibility of exercising leadership regardless of our job titles. Perhaps your boss asked you what you expected from a leader when they first hired you. What if you asked that question of yourself now?

Perhaps contemplating becoming the leader you have been waiting for gives you pause. Great leaders, you say, have a certain something that you are not sure you have. Fredrick is the CEO of a nonprofit organization that dedicates itself to improving the lives of consumers and societies across the globe. Wearing his sleeves rolled-up, he walks into the room with an easy and upright confidence. He speaks directly, in a clipped northwestern European accent that is immediately endearing. For him, the distinction between *leader* and *manager* boils down to charisma; and that charisma is not easily taught. Project management, time management, communication, and resource planning—on the other hand—are all skills any leader could learn when they are learning to become a good manager. If leadership is built on charisma, charisma is built on authenticity, he says. But does that mean that authenticity (charisma or leadership) cannot be developed?

Social work researcher Brené Brown has conducted decades' worth of qualitative research into shame and its interplay with vulnerability[279] and leadership.[280] With the premise that humans are wired for connection and wanting to understand it better, Brown interviewed hundreds of subjects and discovered a funny thing. When she asked about connection, people responded with stories about alienation. When she asked about loving acceptance, people responded with stories about blinding rejection. Her data itself told a fascinating story: Vulnerability was at the core of both shame and courage, creativity and connection. Speaking to a group of people from the American special operations forces, Brown asked the question, "Is courage possible with uncertainty, risk, and emotional exposure?" The reply was that courage was indeed *impossible* without them. The reply confirmed there is no courage—no leadership—without vulnerability and authenticity. Furthermore, courage is just as contagious as fear and scarcity, says Brown. Sharing our stories of overcoming failure is how we scale courage to an organization. The opposite? Lead by fear. Weaponize uncertainty and create scapegoats[281] like you might see in poorly handled corporate regime change. It is temptingly easy to blame the departing leadership and restructure teams and departments to quickly consolidate power by weaponizing the uncertainty of the past.

Fear, however, has a short shelf life. Jacqueline is a policy advisor at a small advocacy group, and she says the trick with leading with fear is creating dependencies, like some religious sects, gangs, or drug cartels. Dependencies on access to food, shelter, and other necessities or benefits can institutionalize rule by fear when fear is no longer the main driver. Benefits, bonuses, and promotions are doled out just like political favors in a corrupt campaign. To the contrary, if we are willing to own our vulnerability, behave and speak our values, connect and nurture trust, own and learn from our failures, we will find ourselves walking the path of the leaders we want to become. In the other words, authenticity can absolutely be developed, but we have to be prepared to practice vulnerability.

Walk the path of leadership and you might also find yourself on a management track. Regardless of whether being the boss was always your goal or merely the unwanted consequence of your positive contributions (the price for you to influence your team's direction), one thing is universal. Power magnifies—rather than hides—the character of the person wielding it. This makes the appointment of a manager a critical decision for a company, but it also means there has been no better time for you to take stock.

Diego is the young manager of a small team of developers in a much larger corporate structure. He was initially reluctant to throw his hat in the ring when a management post opened up in his company until he felt encouragement by his previous managers. After landing the job and despite his apprehension, Diego was determined to give it his all. He studied up on IT management trends and change management from books like *How to Make Your One-on-Ones with Employees More Productive*[282] and videos like Camille Fournier's keynote speech at Linux entitled "Building and Motivating Engineering Teams."[283] With over fifteen thousand books on leadership out there,[284] he focused on leaders within his industry and recommendations from trusted mentors. Fournier in particular spoke about the importance of exercising both the level of technical skill required to inspire confidence from highly trained direct reports and the depth of humility that management needs in order to maintain the space and the safety a team requires to do great work.

After talking to Diego, I was curious to hear the input of my work wife Didi and businesswoman Ilaria. Did they think it was possible for a great leader in management to be both humble and confident? Having met plenty of managers who exuded exceptional confidence without the necessary competence to support it, Ilaria opened by saying, "Confidence and competence are not the same thing, of course." A great boss, particularly at the middle management level, still needed to be technically good. Didi added, "I'd go one further and say that what's more essential than confidence is security—the security in one's self to be able to be challenged and take on questions not as attacks but as ways to improve." They concluded that only a secure leader can serve, not just drive, their team, and security was the result of both confidence and humility.

Service is another key component of great leadership. About the role of service in leadership, South African politician Nelson Mandela said:

It is better to lead from behind and to put others in front, especially when you celebrate victory when nice things occur. You take the front line when there is danger. Then people will appreciate your leadership.[285]

An advisor to Barack Obama would later unnerve conservative circles with the use of the phrase "leading from behind" in regard to the Obama administration's approach to Libya.[286] Simon Sinek in his book *Leaders Eat Last*[287] discusses service as an essential quality to leadership. It features a foreword by a United States Marine Corps general, who notes that at mealtimes senior officers are always served after their junior colleagues:

> *No order is given. Marines just do it. At the heart of this very simple action is the Marine Corps' approach to leadership. Marine leaders are expected to eat last. Because the true price of leadership is the willingness to place the needs of others above your own.*

The commonality between the two concepts of serving our teams first and leading from behind is the notion of service. Leadership implies both the burden and the privilege of leading, of lighting the path for those we lead. As we discussed in Chapter 4: Toxic Work Culture: It Takes Just One Rotten Apple to Spoil the Barrel, there is a complex exchange that occurs between leaders and the teams that follow them. Just as might be seen in a group of primates or other mammals, a leader is given a special place in a tribe. They are the strongest, the bravest, and they receive first dibs on food, home, and mates. But, in return, their tribe expects them to be the first to sacrifice their safety by running to the front lines of battle. A good leader, as we have discussed, provides a level of safety to the team, whether in taking the brunt of a harsh critique from upper management or in ensuring a harassment-free workplace. Sinek posits[288] that leaders protect their tribe by reinforcing positive relationships. The neurotransmitter oxytocin plays a hand in these by providing a biochemical feedback loop that makes us desire these positive interactions, in the same way we might desire the warming feeling of a good bit of chocolate, kissing, or breastfeeding. The system works. The tribe survives, and roles are institutionalized.

When talking about what technical teams require from their managers, Camille Fournier discusses another key prerequisite for a high-performing team: safety. Simply put, a feeling of psychological safety in a team is an essential ingredient for a high-performing team. Leaders in management drive highly performing teams because they have created an environment in which failure is not only possible but invited. No ideas are banned, so brainstorming can be as innovative as the imaginations and spirits of the team members allow.

The truth is, nothing replaces a great leader. Nothing. You can never forget your past leaders and mentors who believed in you, pushed you, helped you become who are today—someone who is getting ready to be that great leader for someone else.

Remember Diego who was reluctant to throw his hat in the ring to become boss? His first thoughts about management were about doing better in the wake of others' failures. "You're scared, that's good. It means that this new role matters to you," I replied. "The bar is still pretty low, though," he laughed, but agreed that he was not trying to compete with others as much as to meet his own standards. He wanted to be an excellent manager who was approachable, competent, and maybe even able to inspire his team to better things, the kind of leader that becomes a mentor. In order to be well prepared for his new duties, he took steps to become prepared ahead of his first day in the office.

Diego asked his supervisors about the new workplan so that

he could align his team strategy and identify quick wins for the first year. He needed to clarify workflows and approval processes like contract extensions, promotions, leave management, objective-setting, and performance review. He also wanted to determine what training opportunities were at his disposal, both for his own use and the further development of his team members. He even wondered whether handing his team a book about communication would help them with conflict resolution, reminiscent of Microsoft's Satya Nadella handing his new executive team the 2003 book *Nonviolent Communication* by the psychologist Marshall B. Rosenberg.[289]

Kathy, a new manager in communications, had a very different introduction to her new duties. "You've got what seems like double the work immediately, without the trust set up for you to start delegating wholeheartedly. Your team has their own complicated spider's web of negative and positive relationships, which might affect performance, and don't forget the goals and expectations you are expected to set before you have understood what your team actually does."

She continued, over our bagel sandwiches: "And maybe it's time to fire someone. Or you just lost a star performer, maybe someone who wanted your job but whom the team relied on. You've got a new slot to hire for, which takes hours of deep consideration while other managers look at you slant-eyed in fear you want to poach someone from their team. You want to ask for help, and you should. But it's not easy." Eventually Kathy found the resources she needed and honed her leadership style to become a respected woman in her field, but she regretted the lack of support. Everyone seemed racked with the fear of being found insufficient, and it was crippling their performance, including hers.

Despite our best efforts, there is a learning curve we can expect as new managers. According to *Forbes*,[290] 60% of first-time managers underperform in their first two years. The primary reason is obvious: Management is a skillset in and of itself. You have to learn it, and there are several steps you can take to encourage early success, including determining how you wish to present yourself to your team in accordance with corporate culture and social limits. You may want to ascertain what resources and training are available to help you learn how to manage people, especially within your organization.[291] It is taken for granted that new hires will have read the company's manuals and policies. In addition, there are blogs, books, and various informal fora as well as corporate management training. Another key to success is deciding early on that you will consider your team's mistakes to be your mistakes. Instead of punishing mistakes with shame or placing sole blame, treat mistakes like teaching opportunities for the entire team. These tactics are not nice-to-haves; they are essential elements that a new manager should bring to a team. *Forbes* states that a good manager can increase an employee's commitment to their job by 34%.[292] Focus on creating the right space for performance, even if that means answering phones while your colleague works on perfecting the slides for your team's next big presentation. No job should be too small when your team's success is on the line.

New Manager Sanity Check

You have the proverbial one hundred days hanging over your head in which you have to prove yourself, but that is no excuse to run without looking.

- ☐ Listen to your former/new teammates/supervisors.

- Accept you do not have the whole picture. Ask about expectations, frustrations, and wins.
- ☐ Set up one-on-ones. You have two eyes and one mouth; listen twice as hard as you talk. Ignoring the unit for the sake of the individuals will be costly.
- ☐ Do not ignore tricky team dynamics. You might be managing former peers or perhaps someone who was refused for your job. Find occasions to foster the kind of comradery that supports trust; spring for the bubbles.
- ☐ Your team (and colleagues) may have erroneous expectations of you based on your gender, race, sexual orientation, or experience. Do not bury your fears under a rug. Seek out other managers in similar circumstances. You may need support, and nothing speaks quite as strongly as experience.
- ☐ Do not forget to manage up! You might have one of the hardest jobs in the company, especially if you are a middle manager, but your boss also needs to be on track with your team's performance. Showcase your team's performance with pride while ensuring you highlight the individuals.
- ☐ Finally, do not neglect yourself. A lack of support and mentoring is one of the many complaints[293] young managers face. You may feel unhealthy and warrantless pressure to perform. Recognize that pressure for what it is, and seek out resources and support.

Mahatma Gandhi has been quoted as having said, "A man is but the product of his thoughts; what he thinks, he becomes."[294] Whether you are a new manager, want to become one, or simply wish to take more ownership over your work, recasting your self-image against the relief of authenticity, vulnerability, service, and structured management might take you out of yourself and inspire you to want to be more. If one person's recipe for great leadership says take a drop of vulnerability with a strong dollop of purpose and shake it in a decanter of experience, your recipe might entail something altogether different. What matters—in the words of American drag queen RuPaul—is that "when you become the image of your own imagination, it's the most powerful thing you could ever do."[295]

CHAPTER FOURTEEN: WHEN EVERYTHING ELSE HAS FAILED…

…happiness depends on ourselves…

—ARISTOTLE (J. A. K. THOMSON TRANSLATION)[296]

Born in 1926 and versed in art, anthropology, and psychology, David Steindl-Rast cuts a thin, gentle line in his simple monk's robes as he speaks in a Viennese accent before a large auditorium of TED Talk attendees:

What is the connection between happiness and gratefulness? Many people would say, well, that's very easy. When you are happy, you are grateful. But think again. Is it really the happy people that are grateful? We all know quite a number of people who have everything that it would take to be happy, and they are not happy, because they want something else or they want more of the same. And we all know people who *have lots of misfortune, misfortune that we ourselves would not want to have, and they are deeply happy. They radiate happiness. You are surprised. Why? Because they are grateful. So it is not happiness that makes us grateful. It's gratefulness that makes us happy.[297]*

Over decades and across countries, Steindl-Rast has taught gratefulness with the conviction that it has the power to revolutionize the world. He suggests a simple exercise of "stop, look, and go" that resembles the mindfulness we practiced in Chapter 12: Deciding to Stay and Pursue Perfection. Gratefulness, however, seems to go one step further.

Steindl-Rast says that happiness rises spontaneously in our hearts along with gratefulness when we receive something both valuable and freely given. He emphasizes that the valuable thing must be truly given; we have not bought it, earned it, or traded it in. Moreover, we can find the opportunity in every given moment, at the very least, because we have it and even if we miss the opportunity, another moment comes before another, freely, without guarantee or control. The foundation of his gospel of gratitude is the belief that gratitude is powerful because gratefulness eliminates fear, and without fear, we act out of a sense of having and being enough, not of scarcity. We are willing to share, to respect others and our differences. We are living gratefully.

What does it mean to choose to find joy or happiness in our work each day?

Ilaria, whom we met in Chapter 9: Mentorship—The Secret Ingredient to a Great Career, starts her day deliberately choosing to be happy, deciding to find the good in each moment. An analytical businesswoman, she could take the approach of other intelligent people toward cynicism, but instead, in the way that the truly gifted are often hidden behind a humble, wide-eyed curiosity about the world, her mind runs to the good, the constructive, the happy. She adds, "But it's not a simple practice. It's not easy. It takes effort and training."

Happiness is a word laden with connotations and denotations. The comic strip *The Oatmeal*[298] starts off by saying, "I am not a happy person." The narrator mocks the definition of happiness as an all-encompassing, perfectly satiating state of completion, an impossible Buddha-like nirvana that confabulates the different elements of knowing no want or suffering and having every want or desire met. The comic goes on to confess that this definition "isn't very good. It's a monochromatic word used to describe a rich, painful spectrum of human feeling."[299]

Then the narrator does something interesting. He talks of his love of running despite losing toenails, working to the point of missing food and hygiene breaks in a buoying addictive state of "flow," and reading and learning about wonders from the complex to the simply mundane. He concludes that he does not want to be "happy"; he wants to be interested, engaged, and curious, with or without an element of suffering.

Over the course of your life, experiences will have shaped the various meanings that "happy" has for you—from primal pleasure to a self-loathing indictment of scarcity. Perhaps you prefer "flow" or "joy" or "satisfaction" or "fulfillment." I am not sure that the word itself is as important as conveying the idea of a desired state of full engagement and purpose. It lies at the corner of knowing what you want and having it. It is where you refuel.

When I ask Ilaria what makes her happy, she answers

simply: "the possibility to work with happy people." She deeply enjoys when her work brings people together and gives them satisfaction. I wondered if there might be a theme behind this response, so I also asked around. I got answers from everyone from interns to senior directors and from the miserable to the delighted. No one said money made them happy. Instead, their following replies centered around various themes: (1) working with good people, (2) feeling seen and valued, and (3) contributing to a greater whole, feeling inspired and productive. Often the comments doubled or tripled on themes. See if any resonate for you.

Working with a Good Boss/Team

"Autonomy over my work and how I handle it. Colleagues I get along with. Quiet working environment. Variety in the work. Problem solving (and supportive colleagues around problems). Recognition of the work I've done (I don't need or want public recognition, just a 'You did good' would be awesome)."—an IT expert

"I need to achieve things and work with smart people."—a newly minted manager

"Exciting work, great coworkers, a boss who believes in me and my potential."—an HR professional

"Feeling like what I am doing is making a difference. Not on a higher ethical level, just basically that what I do moves the team forward, not backward."—an attorney

Feeling Seen and Valued

"[Bad timing for this question, ha!] Seriously though… I guess for me having reliable and relatable coworkers makes doing anything more enjoyable. Doing work without human connection is kind of boring. So, the human contact, whether [that] is emails to members, just chatting over a coffee, or in a project setting, that's most worthwhile."—a policy advocate

"Feeling useful and lovely colleagues!"—a communications manager

"Coworkers (good atmosphere at work); days that are full of interesting (if possible) things to do (I hate to be bored). Recognition of the work done by peers and management. Knowing that what I do 'makes sense' (or has an impact somewhere)."—a business analyst

"Feeling useful."—a tax lawyer

Contributing to a Greater Whole

"When I am doing something that I know will either be meaningful or demonstrate through providing evidence meaning within the organization or optimize and ease future work."—a data scientist

"Having challenging things to work on. Always facing new topics and learning new things. Having the freedom to organize my work almost as I want. The good relationship I have (most of the time) with my boss. The feeling of working for a company with a meaning…the pleasure to work with great people. Having the feeling of being useful. Feeling that people trust me and that I am not such a bad manager."—an IT manager

"Sounds cliché but: Seeing people grow in their jobs. Having a positive influence on people. Being part of something bigger than oneself. Being part of a team."—a legal manager

"Straightforward but difficult question! For me, it would be to work with and for people, i.e., knowing that what I did made a difference for someone. Secondly, solving a complex problem. Thirdly, struggling and producing a really excellent piece of work. Finally, being able to produce the last-mentioned under immense pressure!"—a director

....

Perhaps you too heard yourself in some of these replies. Asking this simple question—What makes you happy at work?—had a penetrative effect on my conversations that I did not expect, regardless of how the speaker felt about the job they held. There was a funny kind of pause each time after I asked the question—the kind of pause that makes the answer feel more important.

Happiness might mean different things to different people, but what does it mean to companies? Money. With leaders like Google and Goldman-Sachs, companies are starting to pay more and more attention to the happiness of their employees. According to a study by Warwick University from 2009,[300] positivity can boost productivity by 12%. Its inverse? Negativity in the workplace can dampen productivity by as much as 10%.[301] As Brené Brown states in *Braving the Wilderness*:

> *When the culture of any organization mandates that it is more important to protect the reputation of a system and those in power than it is to protect the basic human dignity of the individuals who serve that system or who are served by that system, you can be certain that the shame is systemic, the money is driving ethics, and the accountability is all but dead. [302]*

After a certain pay-threshold, employees are generally more driven by autonomy, company culture, values, and the feeling of being appreciated and respected. On the face of it, it seems that these "soft factors" are all cost-neutral and should be easy goals for companies to meet. In practice, however, they can be exceptionally expensive when you consider how much time is spent in consulting and strategizing, the resources expended in attracting, developing, and retaining the right kind of candidates and employees, and the efforts required to cut ties with staff who are unwilling to change their toxic ways.

Google has famously spent a pretty penny investing in the happiness of its workers. It invested time and money for an external researcher to examine its high-performing teams and to discover what their link was. They found that safety was a precursor in every single one—above having complementary aptitudes and attitudes. Moreover, Google has poured money into its campuses, featuring free food and classes, open gyms, and talks from thought-leaders.[303] A more cynical view might be that it is just an attempt to entice workers to stay on campus for longer and longer hours. Either way, however, Google saw an increase of 37% in employee support and satisfaction.

Forbes presents the argument for boosting employee satisfaction from a profitability standpoint, highlighting a University of Tennessee study[304] of the employee-friendly (EF) cultures of 3,446 companies from forty-three countries between 2003 and 2014. The researchers found that companies with a high EF culture reaped higher profitability and return on assets, in part because of their increased, measurable innovation and efficiency.[305] Additionally, companies with a high EF culture rating performed much better before, during, and after the Great Recession, suggesting that the power of a happy workforce provides a buffer even in the most severe of wider economic circumstances. Unsurprisingly, good corporate governance proved to be key because it imbues an employee culture with effective values; but beware of copying and pasting from another company's value charter: "Setting the right tone comes from the board of directors' and senior management's willingness to behave in a manner consistent with what they demand from other employees."[306] In other words, "do what I do" is a lot more important than "do what I say" when it comes to maintaining an EF culture.

Whether you prefer workplace perks like free food, open gyms, and interactive workspaces or employee benefits that enrich your life outside the office, like gym subscriptions, transportation, and childcare subsidies, only you can decide which corporate culture is a good fit for your needs. While data can help our companies understand the factors at play in making us happy, no poll, survey, or board decision can substitute us answering that question for ourselves. Perhaps it is in the practice of gratefulness that we find that answer, but it is also in each other.

With a finger still on the trackpad and your chin on your palm, you might be lucky enough to glance at happiness flickering across your colleague's face as she closes the first meeting she has ever led. Or, perhaps, in remembering your workmate's story about struggling to avoid black ice last winter, when you ask him today about his cold ride to work, he will blush in happy acknowledgement that in some small way, you see him. What a simple joy it is to pour yourself a coffee and silently reminisce about your exceptional colleagues and their wonderful stories, so many of them told over that first morning coffee when they were shaking off their frenetic morning and bracing themselves for the day ahead. Sometimes that morning's *bonjour* or good morning can be the first opportunity to practice gratefulness and boost the employee-friendly culture at work that you want to see.

Finally, a good dose of humility can help us in trying to make the kind of meaningful connections at work that boost our happiness. Sometimes blind to our colleagues' viewpoints, we can fall victim to thinking we have all the answers or the best perspective. We have all been in that meeting with someone who thought he or she was the smartest person in the room. So, when we walk into a room, ready to dismiss half or more of what we hear, let us remember that others can feel it, too. We convey information through our glances, facial expressions, and body language in addition to our mere words, verbal tone, or spacing.[307] When we practice humility, we listen more, speak less, and mirror our colleagues' body language. We might even notice hidden agendas, recalcitrant pauses, disagreement in turned heads, and allies in sustained eye contact. We connect.

We often connect in the off-the-clock moments when we let down our guard and share stories from our weekend or favorite recipes or athletic teams. We build trust and communication on the back of that intimacy and vulnerability; and, ultimately, we find that our work, no matter how great or how small in the grand scheme of things, has meaning when that work has meaning for others.

In the prologue, I told you I broke the cardinal rule of not quitting a great job, and then I broke another by telling you how this book would end. It all comes down to connection. Just as gratefulness has the power to replace the fear of scarcity with sating happiness, connection is the cornerstone of a healthy, productive workplace, and in turn, a fulfilling career; but this kind of connection requires us each to do our part. When asked for her most valuable advice, Pulitzer Prize-winning author Dr.

Maya Angelou offered her grandmother's words: "Now sister, you know what's right. Just do right."[308] Sounds simple, right? Maybe it is. It is up to us now to do what is right, to build our armies, and to lead our work lives.

So, I conclude, sheepishly paraphrasing the words[309] of Chilean author Isabel Allende, a woman and writer far wiser and more talented than I: "So tell me, Dear Reader, what is it that you plan to do with your one wild and precious career. Me? I intend to work passionately!"

NOTES

[1] **Chapter One: How Did I Get Here? Making Your Next Career Move**
García Márquez, Gabriel. *Love in the Time of Cholera*. Vintage, 1988, p. 168.

[2] Jarrett, Valerie. "Valerie Jarrett on 26-Year-Old Michelle Obama's Unforgettable Job Interview, and Dinner with a Political Super Couple-to-Be." *Literary Hub*, 4. Apr. 2019, lithub.com/valerie-jarrett-on-26-year-old-michelle-obamas-unforgettable-job-interview/.

[3] Obama, Michelle. *Becoming*. Crown, 2018, p. 1.

[4] Krumboltz, John D. "The Happenstance Learning Theory." *Journal of Career Assessment*, vol. 1.7.2 (2009): 135-154. *SAGE Journals*, journals.sagepub.com/doi/abs/10.1177/1069072708328861.

[5] Krumboltz also advocates for career assessment tools that help to stimulate understanding, as opposed to simply pigeonholing people, in addition to being honest with yourself about your own willingness to explore he calls "beneficial unplanned events," i.e., how willing are you to take a risk on an unexpected opportunity?

[6] Stanford University. "How people choose 'career paths'." *Stanford University News Release*, 28 May 1991. news.stanford.edu/pr/91/910528Arc1355.html. Accessed 20 Nov. 2019.

[7] Stahl, Ashley. "5 Steps to Finding the Right Career for You." *Forbes*, 27 Sep. 2018, www.forbes.com/sites/ashleystahl/2018/09/27/5-steps-to-finding-the-right-career-for-you/#56cd470e5abb.

[8] Berger, Guy. "Will This Year's College Grads Job-Hop More Than Previous Grads?" *LinkedIn Official Blog*, LinkedIn, 12 Apr. 2016, blog.linkedin.com/2016/04/12/will-this-year_s-college-grads-job-hop-more-than-previous-grads.

[9] Long, Heather. "The new normal: 4 job changes by the time you're 32." *CNN Business*, 12 Apr. 2016, money.cnn.com/2016/04/12/news/economy/millennials-change-jobs-frequently/index.html.

[10] To preserve their privacy, many interviewees' names have been changed.

[11] Stahl, Ashley. "5 Steps to Finding the Right Career for You." *Forbes*, 27 Sep. 2018, www.forbes.com/sites/ashleystahl/2018/09/27/5-steps-to-finding-the-right-career-for-you/#56cd470e5abb.

[12] Pullman, George. *A Rulebook for Decision Making*. Massachusetts: Hackett Publishing Company, 2015, p. 91.

[13] Idem.

[14] Palmer, Amanda. "The Art of Asking." *TED*, Feb. 2013, www.ted.com/talks/amanda_palmer_the_art_of_asking?language=en. See also Palmer, Amanda. *The art of asking, or, How I learned to stop worrying and let people help*. Rand Central Publishing, 2014.

[15] Winfrey, Oprah. "Winfrey's Commencement Address." Harvard University, *Harvard Gazette*, 31 May 2013, news.harvard.edu/gazette/story/2013/05/winfreys-commencement-address/.

Chapter Two: This is Not Your Dad's Midlife Crisis

[16] Alighieri, Dante. *The Divine Comedy: Volume 1 Inferno*. Translated by Mark Musa, Penguin Classics, 2003, p. 67.

[17] Jaques, Elliott. "Death and the Midlife Crisis." *International Journal of Psychoanalysis*, 1965, pp. 502-14

[18] "Life Expectancy at Birth, Total (Years)." *The World Bank*, 3 Dec. 2019, data.worldbank.org/indicator/SP.DYN.LE00.IN.

[19] Jaques gives no basis for this hypothesis that midlife was connected to declining sexuality. Additionally, the notion of lifetime sexual peaks and valleys is a complex one, including whether number of orgasms, physical fitness for arousal, or personal perceptions of the quality of sexual activity are used as benchmarks. The myth that men's and women's sexual peak is in their teenage years and thirties, respectively, has been questioned by various studies depending on which benchmark was used, leading some to conclude that the best sex of your life is not pinned to a specific age as much as a specific relationship. See McGowan, Emma. "This Is When You Reach Your Sexual Peak." *Bustle*, Bustle Digital Group, 18 Apr. 2017, www.bustle.com/p/when-do-you-reach-your-sexual-peak-heres-what-science-says-50296.

[20] Rothman, Joshua. "The Philosophy of the Midlife Crisis." *The*

New Yorker, 3 Feb. 2018, www.newyorker.com/books/page-turner/the-philosophy-of-the-midlife-crisis.

[21] Setiya, Kieran. *Midlife: A Philosophical Guide*. Princeton University Press, 2018, p 3.

[22] Idem.

[23] Alighieri, Dante. *The Divine Comedy: Volume 1 Inferno.* Translated by Mark Musa, Penguin Classics, 2003, p. 67.

[24] Setiya, Kieran. *Midlife: A Philosophical Guide*. Princeton University Press, 2018, p 9.

[25] Coleridge, Samuel Taylor. "The Rime of the Ancient Mariner." Poetry Foundation, www.poetryfoundation.org/poems/43997/the-rime-of-the-ancient-mariner-text-of-1834.

[26] Steindl-Rast, David. "Want to be happy? Be grateful." *TED*, June 2013, www.ted.com/talks/david_steindl_rast_want_to_be_happy_be_grateful?language=en.

[27] Squires, Sally. "Midlife Without a Crisis." *The Washington Post*, WP Company, 19 Apr. 1999, www.washingtonpost.com/wp-srv/health/seniors/stories/midlife042099.htm??noredirect=on. See also "Research Network on Successful Midlife Development." *MacArthur Foundation*, 3 Dec. 2019, www.macfound.org/networks/research-network-on-successful-midlife-development/details/.

[28] "Life Expectancy at Birth, Total (Years)." *The World Bank*, 3 Dec. 2019, data.worldbank.org/indicator/SP.DYN.LE00.IN.

[29] Blanchflower, David G. and Andrew J. Oswald. "Is well-being U-shaped over the life cycle?" *Social Science & Medicine*, vol. 66, 2008, pp. 1733-49. Dartmouth University, www.dartmouth.edu/~blnchflr/papers/welbbeingssm.pdf.

[30] The list of seventy-two countries surveyed showed an enviable comprehensiveness: Argentina, Australia, Azerbaijan, Belarus, Belgium, Bosnia, Brazil, Brunei, Bulgaria, Cambodia, Canada, Chile, China, Colombia, Costa Rica, Croatia, Czech Republic, Denmark, Dominican Republic, Ecuador, El Salvador, Estonia, Finland, France, Germany, Greece, Honduras, Hungary, Iceland, Iraq, Ireland, Israel, Italy, Japan, Kyrgyzstan, Laos, Latvia, Lithuania, Luxembourg, Macedonia, Malta, Mexico, Myanmar, Netherlands, Nicaragua, Nigeria, Norway, Paraguay, Peru, Philippines, Poland, Portugal, Puerto Rico, Romania, Russia, Serbia, Singapore, Slovakia, South Africa, South Korea, Spain, Sweden, Switzerland, Tanzania, Turkey, the United

Kingdom, Ukraine, Uruguay; the United States, Uzbekistan, and Zimbabwe. See idem.

[31] Using European averages does mask interesting national differences for when well-being was reported to be lowest, such as 35.8 in the United Kingdom versus 66.1 in Portugal, and France and Spain in the middle at 49.5 and 50.1, respectively. Without drawing conclusions, the authors pointed to the cohort effect, that a group of people may be more or less happy because of external political, economic, and historic factors.

[32] Calhoun, Ada. "The New Midlife Crisis for Women: Why (and How) It's Hitting Gen X Women." Oprah.com, Harpo, 3 Dec. 2019, www.oprah.com/sp/new-midlife-crisis.html.

[33] David, Patty. "Generation X Snapshots: Health." *AARP Research*, December 2015. doi.org/10.26419/res.00116.000 /life/2015/GenX-Health-Infographic-res-life.pdf

[34] A new caricature of midlife crisis is trending: the CrossFit Daddy training to look like David Beckham. Based on a study from a British healthcare company, health kicks are apparently the most popular expression of midlife crisis. Something about working out until you can beat the records of your twenty-year-old self seems to help stave off the encroaching discomfort of aging. See Lally, Maria. "The New Midlife Crisis: How We Swapped the Sports Car for a Six-Pack." *The Telegraph*, 9 Aug. 2019, www.telegraph.co.uk/health-fitness/body/new-midlife-crisis-swapped-sports-car-six-pack/.

[35] Forbes Coaches Council. "15 Signs You've Hit Your Mid-Life Crisis (And What To Do About It)." *Forbes*, 31 Aug. 2017, www.forbes.com/sites/forbescoachescouncil/2017/08/31/15-signs-youve-hit-your-mid-life-crisis-and-what-to-do-about-it/.

[36] Crace, John. "Surviving the Midlife Crisis: a 10-Point Guide." *The Guardian*, Guardian News and Media, 29 Sept. 2010, www.theguardian.com/society/2010/sep/29/10-point-guide-to-beating-that-midlife-crisis.

Chapter Three: Refocusing the Lens after Disappointment and Facing Yourself

[37] Esquivel, Laura. *Like Water for Chocolate: A Novel in Monthly Instalments with Recipes, Romance and Home Remedies.* Translated by

Carol Christensen and Thomas Christensen. Black Swan, 1993, p 104.

[38] Levchuck, Caroline. "What to Do When You're Passed over for a Promotion at Work." *Business Insider*, 27 Feb. 2018, www.businessinsider.com/what-to-do-when-youre-passed-over-for-a-promotion-at-work-2018-2?r=US&IR=T.

[39] Clance, Pauline Rose and Suzanne Imes. "The Impostor Phenomenon in High Achieving Women: Dynamics and Therapeutic Interventions. *Psychotherapy: Theory Research and Practice*, vol. 15, 1978. www.paulineroseclance.com/pdf/ip_high_achieving_women.pdf

[40] Idem, p 2.

[41] Idem, p 5.

[42] Clance, Pauline Rose. *The Impostor Phenomenon: Overcoming the Fear That Haunts Your Success*. Peachtree Publishers, 1985.

[43] Langford, Joe Langford and Pauline Rose Clance. "The Impostor Phenomenon: Recent Research Findings Regarding Dynamics, Personality and Family Patterns and Their Implications for Treatment." *Psychotherapy*, vol. 30, 1993, no. 3, paulineroseclance.com/pdf/-Langford.pdf.

[44] Idem, p. 496.

[45] Idem, p. 498.

[46] Brown, Brené. "Daring Greatly: How the Courage to be Vulnerable Transforms the Way We Live, Love, Parent, and Lead." Penguin Putnam, 2012.

[47] Lastovkova, Andrea, et al. "Burnout Syndrome as an Occupational Disease in the European Union: An Exploratory Study." *Industrial Health*, National Institute of Occupational Safety and Health, Japan, Mar. 2018, pp. 160-65. www.ncbi.nlm.nih.gov/pmc/articles/PMC5889935/.

[48] Rough, Jenny. "From Moms to Medical Doctors, Burnout Is Everywhere These Days." *The Washington Post*, WP Company, 30 Mar. 2019, www.washingtonpost.com/national/health-science/from-moms-to-medical-doctors-burnout-is-everywhere-these-days/2019/03/29/1cea7d92-401d-11e9-922c-64d6b7840b82_story.html.

[49] "Maslach Burnout Inventory (MBI)—Assessments, Tests: Mind Garden." *Mind Garden*, www.mindgarden.com/117-maslach-burnout-

inventory#horizontalTab3.

[50] Rough, Jenny. "From Moms to Medical Doctors, Burnout Is Everywhere These Days." *The Washington Post*, WP Company, 30 Mar. 2019, www.washingtonpost.com/national/health-science/from-moms-to-medical-doctors-burnout-is-everywhere-these-days/2019/03/29/1cea7d92-401d-11e9-922c-64d6b7840b82_story.html.

[51] "Supplement to Diagnostic and Statistical Manual of Mental Disorders, Fifth Edition." American Psychiatric Association, Oct. 2017, psychiatryonline.org/pb-assets/dsm/update/DSM5Update_October2017.pdf.

[52] Schaufeli, W. B. "Burnout in Europe: Relations with national economy, governance, and culture. Research Unit Occupational & Organizational Psychology and Professional Learning (internal report)." KU Leuven, 2018, wilmarschaufeli.nl/publications/Schaufeli/500.pdf.

[53] zur Nedden, Cristina. "European Founders Suffer from 'Reality Distortion', Burnout and Anxiety." *Sifted*, 17 Apr. 2019, sifted.eu/articles/jorg-rheinboldt-founders-suffer-from-reality-distortion/.

[54] Krystal D'Costa. "Why Aren't We Talking About Burnout?" *Scientific American*, 8 May 2014, blogs.scientificamerican.com/anthropology-in-practice/why-aren-8217-t-we-talking-about-burnout/?redirect=1.

[55] Montero-Marin J, et al. "Coping with Stress and Types of Burnout: Explanatory Power of Different Coping Strategies," *PLOS ONE*, 13 Feb. 2014, journals.plos.org/plosone/article?id=10.1371/journal.pone.0089090.

[56] Joel Stein. "Millennials: The Me Me Me Generation," *Time Magazine*, 20 May 2013, time.com/247/millennials-the-me-me-me-generation/

[57] Pendell, Ryan. "Millennials Are Burning Out." *Gallup*, 19 Nov. 2019, https://www.gallup.com/workplace/237377/millennials-burning.aspx.

[58] Kathy Caprino, "How To Cure Your Burnout Without Quitting Your Job," *Forbes*, 7 Nov. 2014. www.forbes.com/sites/kathycaprino/2014/11/07/how-to-cure-your-burnout-without-quitting-your-job/#358b71ae541a

[59] "Paula Davis-Laack: Resilience Experts." The Stress & Resilience Institute, 12 Sept. 2019, stressandresilience.com/.

Chapter Four: Toxic Work Culture - It Takes Just One Rotten Apple to Spoil the Barrel

[60] "Dr. Maya Angelou on the Power of Words." Angelou, Maya. *OWN*, Oprah's Master Class, 28 May 2014, www.youtube.com/watch?v=BKv65MdlV-c.

[61] Kouvonen, Anne, et al. "Negative Aspects of Close Relationships as a Predictor of Increased Body Mass Index and Waist Circumference: The Whitehall II Study." American Public Health Association, *American Journal of Public Health (AJPH)*, Aug. 2011, ajph.aphapublications.org/doi/full/10.2105/AJPH.2010.300115.

[62] Idem.

[63] Bourg Carter, Sherrie. "Coworkers from Hell! Strategies for Coping with Work Jerks." *Psychology Today*, Sussex Publishers, 11 July 2011, www.psychologytoday.com/us/blog/high-octane-women/201107/coworkers-hell.

[64] Bourg Carter, Sherrie. "The Hidden Health Hazards of Toxic Relationships: Being around a Toxic Friend, Partner, or Co-Worker Can Do Real Damage." *Psychology Today*, Sussex Publishers, 11 Aug. 2011, www.psychologytoday.com/intl/blog/high-octane-women/201108/the-hidden-health-hazards-toxic-relationships.

[65] Sinek, Simon. "Why Good Leaders Make You Feel Safe." *TED*, Mar. 2014, www.ted.com/talks/simon_sinek_why_good_leaders_make_you_feel_safe.

[66] Sinek, Simon. *Leaders Eat Last: Why Some Teams Pull Together and Others Don't*. Penguin Business, 2017.

[67] Social contract theory is roughly based on the idea that the web of individual commitments that keep us safe is the basis of society. Most associated with Thomas Hobbes, John Locke, and Jean-Jacques Rousseau, it is one of the dominant moral and political theories in Western thinking. Recent criticism of the model, including by feminist and race-conscious philosophers, includes that it fails to account for the nuances of subjugation. See Friend, Celeste. "Social Contract Theory." *The Internet Encyclopedia of Philosophy*, www.iep.utm.edu/soc-cont/.

[68] Uvnäs-Moberg, Kerstin. "Oxytocin May Mediate the Benefits of Positive Social Interaction And Emotions." *Psychoneuroendocrinology*, vol. 23, no. 8, Nov. 1998, pp. 819-35., doi:10.1016/s0306-4530(98)00056-0.

[69] Sinek, Simon. *Leaders Eat Last: Why Some Teams Pull Together and Others Don't.* Penguin Business, 2017, pp. 78-83.

[70] Harari, Yuval Noah. *Sapiens: A Brief History of Humankind.* Vintage, 2011, pp. 27-31.

[71] Sinek, Simon. *Leaders Eat Last: Why Some Teams Pull Together and Others Don't.* Penguin Business, 2017, pp. 65-72.

[72] Irvin-Lazorko, Pamela. "Chronic Stress of Workplace Bullying And Cortisol Response." *Medical News Today*, MediLexicon International, 19 May 2011, www.medicalnewstoday.com/articles/225955.php#1.

[73] Sinek, Simon. *Leaders Eat Last: Why Some Teams Pull Together and Others Don't.* Penguin Business, 2017, pp. 62-64.

[74] Galbally, Megan, et al. "The Role of Oxytocin in Mother-Infant Relations: a Systematic Review of Human Studies." *Harvard Review of Psychiatry*, U.S. National Library of Medicine, 2011, www.ncbi.nlm.nih.gov/pubmed/21250892.

[75] Cappelli, Peter. "Why We Love to Hate HR...and What HR Can Do About It." *Harvard Business Review*, 2015, pp. 54-61., hbr.org/2015/07/why-we-love-to-hate-hr-and-what-hr-can-do-about-it.

[76] Emerson, Tricia. "How to Change A Toxic Culture." *Forbes*, 29 Apr. 2018, www.forbes.com/sites/triciaemerson/2018/04/29/how-to-change-a-toxic-culture/#5828a4bd54c1.

[77] Eades, John. "Research on Hundreds of Companies Showed Toxic Cultures Have These Characteristics." *Inc.com*, 13 Feb. 2018, www.inc.com/john-eades/research-on-hundreds-of-companies-showed-that-toxic-cultures-have-these-characteristics.html.

[78] Troyani, Laura. "3 Examples of Organizational Change Done Right." *TINYpulse*, 19 Aug. 2019, www.tinypulse.com/blog/3-examples-of-organizational-change-and-why-they-got-it-right.

[79] Abadi, Mark. "When CEO Satya Nadella First Joined Microsoft, He Started Diffusing Its Toxic Culture by Handing Every One of His Execs a 15-Year-Old Book by a Psychologist." *Business Insider*, 3 Oct. 2018, www.businessinsider.in/When-CEO-Satya-Nadella-first-joined-Microsoft-he-started-diffusing-its-toxic-culture-by-handing-every-one-of-his-execs-a-15-year-old-book-by-a-psychologist/articleshow/66060306.cms.

[80] Eichenwald, Kurt. "How Microsoft Lost Its Mojo: Steve Ballmer and Corporate America's Most Spectacular Decline." *Vanity Fair*, 30

Jan. 2015, www.vanityfair.com/news/business/2012/08/microsoft-lost-mojo-steve-ballmer.

[81] Sherr, Ian. "This Is Not Your Father's Microsoft." *CNET*, 30 Aug. 2018, www.cnet.com/news/this-is-not-your-fathers-microsoft/.

Chapter Five: A Smiling Face Hides a Hissing Snarl - Discrimination Today

[82] "Unpacking White Privilege and Prejudice." *Red Table Talk*, Facebook Watch, http://www.facebook.com/redtabletalk/posts/760598157672995.

[83] Premack, Rachel. "14 Things People Think Are Fine to Say at Work —but Are Actually Racist, Sexist, or Offensive." *Business Insider*, 10 Sept. 2018, www.businessinsider.com/microaggression-unconscious-bias-at-work-2018-6?r=US&IR=T.

[84] Jahangir, Rumeana. "How Does Black Hair Reflect Black History?" *BBC News*, 31 May 2015, www.bbc.com/news/uk-england-merseyside-31438273.

[85] "The Afro-Colombian Journalist Facing Abuse over Her Hair." *BBC News*, 22 May 2019, www.bbc.com/news/av/world-latin-america-48355471/the-afro-colombian-journalist-facing-abuse-over-her-hair.

[86] Recognizing that "ethnic classifications for African decent populations are often vaguely defined, and the concepts underlying them are poorly understood," I am using the term Afro-textured hair to encompass curly hair ranging from wavy Type 2 (a, b, c) to kinky, tight curly Type 4 (a, b, c) hair. See Agyemang, Charles, et al. "Negro, Black, Black African, African Caribbean, African American or What? Labelling African Origin Populations in the Health Arena in the 21st Century." *Journal of Epidemiology & Community Health*, BMJ Publishing Group Ltd, 1 Dec. 2005, jech.bmj.com/content/59/12/1014, and Jordan, Andrea. "How to Determine Your Natural Hair Type." *Oprah Magazine*, 20 Nov. 2019, www.oprahmag.com/beauty/hair/a29858581/natural-hair-types/.

[87] Pruitt, Sarah. "What Part of Africa Did Most Slaves Come from?" *History.com*, A&E Television Networks, 3 May 2016, www.history.com/news/what-part-of-africa-did-most-slaves-come-from.

[88] Gabbert, Wolfgang. "The longue durée of Colonial Violence in Latin America." Historical Social Research / Historische Sozialforschung, Controversies around the Digital Humanities, vol. 37, no. 3 (141), 2012,

pp. 254-75.

[89] Nasheed, Jameelah. "When Black Women Were Required by Law to Cover Their Hair." *Vice*, 10 Apr. 2018, broadly.vice.com/en_us/article/j5abvx/black-womens-hair-illegal-tignon-laws-new-orleans-louisiana.

[90] Gordon, A. "'He's So Articulate.' What That Really Means." *The Root*, 12 Jan. 2017, www.theroot.com/he-s-so-articulate-what-that-really-means-1790874985.

[91] http://theconversation.com/how-the-right-wing-press-has-weaponised-the-ability-to-speak-english-101418

[92] Premack, Rachel. "14 Things People Think Are Fine to Say at Work —but Are Actually Racist, Sexist, or Offensive." *Business Insider*, 10 Sept. 2018, www.businessinsider.com/microaggression-unconscious-bias-at-work-2018-6?r=US&IR=T.

[93] Martínez Pizarro, Jorge, et al. "Tendencias y Patrones De La Migración Latinoamericana y Caribeña Hacia 2010 y Desafíos Para Una Agenda Regional." *Repositorio.cepal.org*, Centro Latinoamericano y Caribeño De Demografía (CELADE)-División De Población De La Comisión Económica Para América Latina y El Caribe (CEPAL), Oct. 2014, repositorio.cepal.org/bitstream/handle/11362/37218/1/S1420586_es.pdf.

[94] "U.S. Census Bureau QuickFacts: United States." *Census Bureau QuickFacts*, www.census.gov/quickfacts/fact/table/US/IPE120217.

[95] Cohen, Richard B. "'Pretty People Always Win': Beauty Bias In The Workplace." *Above the Law*, 6 Apr. 2017, abovethelaw.com/2017/04/pretty-people-always-win-beauty-bias-in-the-workplace/.

[96] Lavery, Daniel M. "Help! I Think My Co-Worker's Weight Is Impeding Her Career. Should I Say Something?" *Slate Magazine*, Slate, 19 Mar. 2019, slate.com/human-interest/2019/03/coworker-weight-workplace-discrimination-advice.html.

[97] Burns, Crosby. "The Costly Business of Discrimination; The Economic Costs of Discrimination and the Financial Benefits of Gay and Transgender Equality in the Workplace." *Center for American Progress*, 22 Mar. 2012, www.americanprogress.org/issues/lgbtq-rights/reports/2012/03/22/11234/the-costly-business-of-discrimination/. See also cdn.americanprogress.org/wp-content/uploads/issues/2012/03/pdf/lgbt_biz_discrimination.pdf

[98] Idem.

[99] Badgett, M. V. "The Economic Costs of Homophobia & the Exclusion of LGBT People: A Case Study in India." Worldbank.org, World Bank, Feb. 2014, www.worldbank.org/content/dam/Worldbank/document/SAR/economic-costs-homophobia-lgbt-exlusion-india.pdf.

[100] Still a Huge Problem." *Vox*, 28 Feb. 2019, www.vox.com/policy-and-politics/2019/2/28/18241973/workplace-discrimination-cpi-investigation-eeoc.

[101]

Chapter Six: Discrimination Focus on the Motherhood Penalty and Fatherhood Bonus Dichotomy

University of Geneva Medical School, *Commission on Equality*, www.unige.ch/medecine/files/9414/5613/9881/PostersMichelleJaeggi_EgaliteOctobre2014.pdf.

[102] "PF2.1. Parental Leave Systems." *Oecd.org*, Organisation for Economic Co-Operation and Development (OECD), Aug. 2019, www.oecd.org/els/soc/PF2_1_Parental_leave_systems.pdf.

[103] "The World Women's Report 2015 Chapter 4 Work." *United Nations*, unstats.un.org/unsd/gender/chapter4/chapter4.html.

[104] Miller, Claire Cain. "The Motherhood Penalty vs. the Fatherhood Bonus," 6 Sept. 2014, www.nytimes.com/2014/09/07/upshot/a-child-helps-your-career-if-youre-a-man.html

[105] Grimshaw, Damian, and Jill Rubery. "The Motherhood Pay Gap: A Review of the Issues, Theory and International Evidence." *International Labour Office*, eige.europa.eu/resources/wcms_371804.pdf.

[106] Saint-Exupéry Antoine de. *The Little Prince*. Translated by Vali Tamm. Houghton Mifflin Harcourt Publishing Company, 2018.

[107] A pivotal comment during the early days of motherhood came from my mother-in-law, who said to me in regard to my work life, "Do what makes you happy. If your babies have a happy mother, they will be happy." Not only have I seen it born out as true, but it was a reflection of the nonjudgmental support all parents, salaried or not, desperately require to be fully productive.

[108] Giudici, Francesco, and Reto Schumacher. "Le Travail Des Mères En Suisse : Évolution Et Déterminants Individuels." *Social Change in Switzerland, N° 10*, www.socialchangeswitzerland.ch/?p=1266.

[109] I was surprised when I learned that in Geneva, despite being the third canton to grant women the right vote regionally, the public-

school system still breaks for lunch under an old mom-stays-home expectation. Luckily, associations have stepped in, as more and more families have working parents and caretakers who cannot pick up their children for lunch during the day. See "13 Key Milestones in the History of Women's Rights in Switzerland." *The Local*, 8 Mar. 2019, www.thelocal.ch/20190308/12-fascinating-facts-about-the-history-of-womens-rights-in-switzerland.

[110] "Married Mothers Less Likely to Participate in Labor Force in 2017 than Other Moms." *U.S. Bureau of Labor Statistics*, 26 Apr. 2018, www.bls.gov/opub/ted/2018/married-mothers-less-likely-to-participate-in-labor-force-in-2017-than-other-moms.htm.

[111] Giudici, Francesco, and Reto Schumacher. "Le Travail Des Mères En Suisse : Évolution Et Déterminants Individuels." *Social Change in Switzerland, N° 10*, www.socialchangeswitzerland.ch/?p=1266.

[112] "The World Women's Report 2015 Chapter 4 Work." United Nations, unstats.un.org/unsd/gender/chapter4/chapter4.html.

[113] Idem.

[114] Tyson, Laura D'Andrea, and Ceri Parker. "An Economist Explains Why Women Are Paid Less." *World Economic Forum*, 8 Mar. 2019, www.weforum.org/agenda/2019/03/an-economist-explains-why-women-get-paid-less/.

[115] Gollayan, Christian. "Stay-at-home moms deserve $160K salary, survey says." *New York Post*, 16 Jan. 2019, nypost.com/2019/01/16/stay-at-home-moms-deserve-160k-salary-survey-says/.

[116] Adams, John. "Clarke Gayford isn't the world's first stay-at-home dad—but he might be the most important," Telegraph, 2 Aug. 2018, www.telegraph.co.uk/family/parenting/clarke-gayford-isnt-worlds-first-stay-at-home-dad-might-important./

[117] Livingston, Gretchen. *"Growing Number of Stay-at-Home Dads."* Pew Research Center's Social & Demographic Trends Project, 5 June 2015, www.pewsocialtrends.org/2014/06/05/growing-number-of-dads-home-with-the-kids/.

[118] Clark, Dorie. "How Stay-at-Home Parents Can Transition Back to Work." *Harvard Business Review*, 24 Apr. 2017, hbr.org/2017/04/how-stay-at-home-parents-can-transition-back-to-work.

[119] Staff at international organizations with permanent positions can enjoy excellent working conditions such as cost-of-living adjustments, children's schooling, housing and transportation

subsidies, and tax-free salaries. It is no surprise they never leave. For temporary contractors, however, working conditions can be miserable with precarious temporary contract situations, no pension or unemployment protection, small salaries, and long hours. See Girardet, Edward. "The United Nations: more consultants, fewer rights." *Le News*, 20 Nov. 2014, lenews.ch/2014/11/20/the-united-nations-more-consultants-fewer-rights/.

[120] Gjersoe, Nathalia. "Bridging the gender gap: why do so few girls study Stem subjects?" *The Guardian*, 8 Mar. 2018, www.theguardian.com/science/head-quarters/2018/mar/08/bridging-the-gender-gap-why-do-so-few-girls-study-stem-subjects.

[121] Tellhed, Una, et al. "Will I Fit in and Do Well? The Importance of Social Belongingness and Self-Efficacy for Explaining Gender Differences in Interest in STEM and HEED Majors." *Sex Roles*, vol. 77, no. 1-2, 29 Oct. 2016, pp. 86-96., link.springer.com/article/10.1007/s11199-016-0694-y#citeas.

[122] Ferrante, Mary Beth. "When Returning to Work, New Mothers Are Lacking Significant Support." *Forbes*, 18 Jan. 2019, www.forbes.com/sites/marybethferrante/2019/01/18/newmoms-return-to-work/#34f26b946190.

Chapter Seven: Corporate Diversity and Inclusion Programs - A Blunted Sword

[123] McDonald, Jordan. "How fighting gender discrimination helped earn Ruth Bader Ginsburg a spot on the Supreme Court." *CNBC make it*, 25 June 2019, www.cnbc.com/2019/06/25/how-ruth-bader-ginsburg-earned-a-supreme-court-nomination.html.

[124] Khomami, Nadia. "#MeToo: How a Hashtag Became a Rallying Cry against Sexual Harassment." *The Guardian*, 20 Oct. 2017, www.theguardian.com/world/2017/oct/20/women-worldwide-use-hashtag-metoo-against-sexual-harassment.

[125] "The #MeToo Moment." Edited by Jessica Bennett, *The New York Times*, www.nytimes.com/series/metoo-moment.

[126] Angèle. "Balance Ton Quoi." Directed by Marx, Jean Claude, YouTube, 15 Apr. 2019, www.youtube.com/watch?v=Hi7Rx3En7-k.

[127] Willsher, Kim. "French Police Issue Almost 450 Fines under Street Harassment Law." *The Guardian*, Guardian News and Media, 30 Apr. 2019, www.theguardian.com/world/2019/apr/30/french-police-issue-almost-450-fines-under-street-harassment-law.

[128] Johnson, Stefanie K., et al. "Has Sexual Harassment at Work Decreased Since #MeToo?" *Harvard Business Review*, 18 July 2019, hbr.org/2019/07/has-sexual-harassment-at-work-decreased-since-metoo.

[129] Dougherty, Debbie S. "The Omissions That Make So Many Sexual Harassment Policies Ineffective." *Harvard Business Review*, 7 July 2017, hbr.org/2017/05/the-omissions-that-make-so-many-sexual-harassment-policies-ineffective.

[130] Gilpin, Lyndsey. "The National Park Service Has a Big Sexual Harassment Problem." *The Atlantic*, Atlantic Media Company, 15 Dec. 2016, www.theatlantic.com/science/archive/2016/12/park-service-harassment/510680/.

[131] Brodesser-akner, Taffy. "The Company That Sells Love to America Had a Dark Secret." *The New York Times*, 23 Apr. 2019, www.nytimes.com/2019/04/23/magazine/kay-jewelry-sexual-harassment.html.

[132] "Herstory." *Black Lives Matter*, blacklivesmatter.com/herstory/.

[133] Mckesson, DeRay. "'I Learned Hope the Hard Way': on the Early Days of Black Lives Matter." *The Guardian*, Guardian News and Media, 12 Apr. 2019, www.theguardian.com/world/2019/apr/12/black-lives-matter-deray-mckesson-ferguson-protests.

[134] McKenzie, Sheena. "Black Lives Matter Protests Spread to Europe." *CNN*, Cable News Network, 11 July 2016, edition.cnn.com/2016/07/11/europe/black-lives-matter-protests-europe/index.html.

[135] Keeanga-Yamahtta Taylor, Keeanga-Yamahtta Taylor, et al. "Five Years Later, Do Black Lives Matter?" *Jacobin*, 30 Sept. 2019, www.jacobinmag.com/2019/09/black-lives-matter-laquan-mcdonald-mike-brown-eric-garner.

[136] One such heated discussion about identity was inadvertently started by Trevor Noah, the South African comedian who was criticized for his joke that Africa had won the World Cup when Frenchman Paul Pogba, of Guinean origins, scored the winning goal for France. The French Ambassador to the US wrote a letter, which Noah read on air, stating that Pogba was a French national playing for, and having learned to play in France, and that to speak of him as an "African" denied his "Frenchness." Noah acknowledged that such denial has been used by extreme right factions to subjugate immigrant

populations but defended his remarks, noting the need for subtlety and context in these discussions, the irony of successful immigrants and their children being claimed "French" but that marginalized and less "savory" immigrants and their children are still considered to "African." He concluded asking why people like Pogba could not be considered *both* French and African: "When I am saying, 'They are African,' I am not saying it as a way to exclude them from their Frenchness but using it as a way to include them in my Africanness." See Noah, Trevor. "Trevor Responds to Criticism from the French Ambassador - Between the Scenes." *The Daily Show*, 18 July 2018, www.youtube.com/watch?v=COD9hcTpGWQ.

[137] Florido, Adrian. "Latino Activists Ask, When Should Brown Lives Matter?" *NPR*, 5 Nov. 2016, www.npr.org/2016/11/05/500810442/latino-activists-ask-when-should-brown-lives-matter?t=1579075540578.

[138] I use colorist here as distinct from race, considering the influence of phenotype: "In the 21st century, as America becomes less white and the multiracial community—formed by interracial unions and immigration—continues to expand, color will be even more significant than race in both public and private interactions. Why? Because a person's skin color is an irrefutable visual fact that is impossible to hide, whereas race is a constructed, quasi-scientific classification that is often only visible on a government form." See Tharps, Lori L. "The Difference Between Racism and Colorism." *Time*, 6 Oct. 2016, time.com/4512430/colorism-in-america/.

[139] Acevedo, Nicole. "White Customer at Mexican Restaurant Swears at Spanish-Speaking Manager." *NBCNews.com*, NBCUniversal News Group, 20 Feb. 2019, www.nbcnews.com/news/latino/white-customer-mexican-restaurant-swears-spanish-speaking-manager-n973191.

[140] Diaz, Johnny. "Woman Ran Over Girl Because She Was 'a Mexican,' Police Say." *The New York Times*, 21 Dec. 2019, www.nytimes.com/2019/12/21/us/Nicole-Marie-Poole-Franklin-Des-Moines.html.

[141] Acevedo, Nicole. "White Customer at Mexican Restaurant Swears at Spanish-Speaking Manager." *NBCNews.com*, NBCUniversal News Group, 20 Feb. 2019, www.nbcnews.com/news/latino/white-customer-mexican-restaurant-swears-spanish-speaking-manager-n973191.

[142] Stack, Liam. "H&M Apologizes for 'Monkey' Image Featuring Black Child." *The New York Times*, 8 Jan. 2018, www.nytimes.com/2018/01/08/business/hm-monkey.html.

[143] Green, Dennis. "Prada is Pulling Monkey-like Trinkets from Stores after Being Accused of Using 'Blackface Imagery'." *Business Insider*, 14 Dec. 2018, www.businessinsider.com/prada-accused-of-blackface-monkey-trinkets-2018-12?r=US&IR=T.

[144] Young, Sarah. "Gucci Apologises for Selling Jumper That 'Resembles Blackface'." *The Independent*, Independent Digital News and Media, 13 Feb. 2019, www.independent.co.uk/life-style/fashion/gucci-blackface-sweater-balaclava-apology-reaction-twitter-controversy-a8767101.html.

[145] Raftery, Brian. "'Saddened' Katy Perry Speaks out on Blackface Shoes Controversy." *Fortune*, 12 Feb. 2019, fortune.com/2019/02/12/katy-perry-blackface-shoes-response/.

[146] Blackface itself was born from the 1800s vaudeville practice of using makeup on White men to supposedly resembled people of African descent by featuring black face paint, exaggerated red lips, and large white eye makeup, to denigrating effect. According to Philip S. S. Howard, Assistant Professor of Education at McGill University, "an obvious problem with blackface is its representational violence—the way in which it openly ridicules Black people [...] it's antiblack." See Howard, Philip S. S. "The Problem with Blackface." *The Conversation*, 11 June 2018, theconversation.com/the-problem-with-blackface-97987.

[147] Mielke, Christine. "Why Do Beauty Brands Resist Diversifying Their Shade Ranges?" *Temptalia*, 5 Dec. 2018, https://www.temptalia.com/why-do-beauty-brands-resist-diversifying-their-shade-ranges/.

[148] Thompson, Sonia. "How Nike, Rihanna, and Procter & Gamble Use Inclusive Marketing to Win More Customers." *Forbes*, 30 Aug. 2018, www.forbes.com/sites/soniathompson/2018/08/30/how-nike-rihanna-and-procter-gamble-use-inclusive-marketing-to-win-more-customers/#7b42c74b7c07.

[149] Idem.

[150] Oster, Erik. "Parents Have 'the Talk' in the Powerful 'My Black Is Beautiful' Campaign From P&G." *Adweek4*, 25 July 2017, https://www.adweek.com/brand-marketing/parents-have-the-talk-in-powerful-my-black-is-beautiful-campaign-from-pg/.

[151] Bourke, Juliet. "How to Be Smarter and Make Better Choices." *TEDxSouthBank*, 25 Apr. 2016, www.youtube.com/watch?v=MZCyUANqYyw.

[152] Pruitt, Allison-Scott, et al. "5 Things We Learned About Creating a Successful Workplace Diversity Program." *Harvard Business Review*, 30 Mar. 2018, hbr.org/2018/03/5-things-we-learned-about-creating-a-successful-workplace-diversity-program.

[153] "Job Patterns for Minorities and Women in Private Industry (EEO-1)." *U.S. Equal Employment Opportunity Commission*, 2018, www.eeoc.gov/eeoc/statistics/employment/jobpat-eeo1/.

[154] "2016 Job Patterns for Minorities and Women in Private Industry (EEO-1)." *U.S. Equal Employment Opportunity Commission*, 2016, www1.eeoc.gov/eeoc/statistics/employment/jobpat-eeo1/2016/index.cfm#select_label.

[155] Elvira, Marta, and Robert Town. "The Effects of Race and Worker Productivity on Performance Evaluations." *Industrial Relations A Journal of Economy and Society*, vol. 40, no. 4, Dec. 2002, pp. 571–590., www.researchgate.net/publication/229683481_The_Effects_of_Race_and_Worker_Productivity_on_Performance_Evaluations.

[156] Dobbin, Frank and Alexandra Kalev. "Why Diversity Programs Fail." *Harvard Business Review*, Jul-Aug 2016, hbr.org/2016/07/why-diversity-programs-fail.

[157] "EEOC Releases Fiscal Year 2018 Enforcement and Litigation Data." *U.S. Equal Employment Opportunity Commission*, 10 Apr. 2019, www.eeoc.gov/eeoc/newsroom/release/4-10-19.cfm.

[158] Dobbin, Frank and Alexandra Kalev. "Why Diversity Programs Fail." *Harvard Business Review*, Jul-Aug 2016, hbr.org/2016/07/why-diversity-programs-fail.

[159] "Household Data Annual Averages." *U.S. Department of Labor Statistics*, 2018, www.bls.gov/cps/cpsaat11.pdf.

[160] Pruitt, Allison-Scott, et al. "5 Things We Learned About Creating a Successful Workplace Diversity Program." *Harvard Business Review*, 30 Mar. 2018, hbr.org/2018/03/5-things-we-learned-about-creating-a-successful-workplace-diversity-program.

[161] Dobbin, Frank and Alexandra Kalev. "Why Diversity Programs Fail." *Harvard Business Review*, Jul-Aug 2016, hbr.org/2016/07/why-diversity-programs-fail.

[162] Bourke, Juliet, and Bernadette Dillon. "The Diversity and Inclusion Revolution: Eight Powerful Truths." *Deloitte Review*, no. 22, Jan. 2018, www2.deloitte.com/content/dam/insights/us/articles/4209_Diversity-and-inclusion-revolution/DI_Diversity-and-inclusion-revolution.pdf.

[163] O'Brien, Michael J. "How to Make Diversity and Inclusion Programs More Effective." *HRExecutive.com*, 5 Dec. 2019, hrexecutive.com/most-di-programs-are-ineffective-heres-how-to-change-that/.

[164] Harris, La'Wana. "Three Derailers Of Diversity and Inclusion (and How To Get Back On Track)." *Forbes*, 13 Dec. 2018, www.forbes.com/sites/forbescoachescouncil/2018/12/13/three-derailers-of-diversity-and-inclusion-and-how-to-get-back-on-track/#e59ce32311c2.

[165] Bourke, Juliet, and Bernadette Dillon. "The Diversity and Inclusion Revolution: Eight Powerful Truths." *Deloitte Review*, no. 22, Jan. 2018, www2.deloitte.com/content/dam/insights/us/articles/4209_Diversity-and-inclusion-revolution/DI_Diversity-and-inclusion-revolution.pdf.

[166] Dobbin, Frank and Alexandra Kalev. "Why Diversity Programs Fail." *Harvard Business Review*, Jul-Aug 2016, hbr.org/2016/07/why-diversity-programs-fail.

Chapter Eight: Behind Every Great (Wo)man Is a Great Work Spouse

[167] Nilles, Billy. "Amy Poehler and Tina Fey's 15 Greatest Moments." *E! Online*, E! News, 1 Oct. 2019, www.eonline.com/news/1078832/the-15-greatest-moments-from-amy-poehler-and-tina-fey-s-friendship.

[168] Cerulo, Erica, and Claire Mazur. *Work Wife: the Power of Female Friendship to Drive Successful Businesses*. Ballantine Books, 2019.

[169] Chapin, Adele. "Bed Bath & Beyond Bought Indie Marketplace of a Kind." *Racked*, 10 Aug. 2015, www.racked.com/2015/8/10/9127225/of-a-kind-bed-bath-beyond.

[170] Cerulo, Erica, and Claire Mazur. "Do You Have a 'Work Wife?' These Founders Think You Should." *Fortune*, 5 Mar. 2019, fortune.com/2019/03/05/work-wife-of-a-kind/.

[171] Idem.

[172] McBride, M. Chad, and Karla Mason Bergen. "Work Spouses: Defining and Understanding a 'New' Relationship." *Communication Studies*, vol. 66, no. 5, *Creighton University*, 15 Aug. 2016, pp.

487–507, creighton.pure.elsevier.com/en/publications/work-spouses-defining-and-understanding-a-new-relationship.

[173] Umoh, Ruth. "Why Scientists Say the Secret to Your Success Could Be Having a 'Work Spouse'." *CNBC Make It*, CNBC, 14 Nov. 2017, www.cnbc.com/2017/11/14/the-secret-to-your-success-could-be-having-a-work-spouse.html.

[174] The most fun was when we would finally put our work away, uncap a few beers, and talk about everything and anything. To wit, I do not know for how long she let me wax on about "A Modest Proposal" being written by English poet Alexander Pope before she gently reminded me that in fact the Anglo-Irish satirist Jonathan Swift had penned the piece.

[175] McBride, M. Chad, and Karla Mason Bergen. "Work Spouses: Defining and Understanding a 'New' Relationship." *Communication Studies*, vol. 66, no. 5, Creighton University, 15 Aug. 2016, pp. 487–507, creighton.pure.elsevier.com/en/publications/work-spouses-defining-and-understanding-a-new-relationship.

[176] Clifford, Catherine. "Why Ben Picked Jerry." *Entrepreneur*, 20 Nov. 2014, www.entrepreneur.com/article/240012.

[177] Wasserman, Noam. "The Founders Dilemmas: Anticipating and Avoiding the Pitfalls That Can Sink a Startup." Princeton University Press, 2012. Also, Wasserman, Noah. "Noam Wasserman: The Founder's Dilemmas." YouTube, Stanford e-Corner, 28 Nov. 2012, www.youtube.com/watch?v=qhmvwOevsSo.

[178] Wasserman, Noam. "The Founder's Dilemma." *Harvard Business Review*, no. February, 2008, hbr.org/2008/02/the-founders-dilemma.

[179] Cross, Rob, et al. "Collaborative Overload." *Harvard Business Review*, no. January-February, 2016, pp. 74–79, https://hbr.org/2016/01/collaborative-overload

[180] Duhigg, Charles. "What Google Learned from Its Quest to Build the Perfect Team." *The New York Times*, 25 Feb. 2016, www.nytimes.com/2016/02/28/magazine/what-google-learned-from-its-quest-to-build-the-perfect-team.html.

[181] Woolley, Anita. "Evidence of a Collective Intelligence Factor in the Performance of Human Groups." *Science*, vol. 330, 29 Oct. 2010, pp. 686-88., www.researchgate.net/publication/47369848_Evidence_of_a_Collective_Intelligence_Factor_in_the_Performance_of_Human_Groups.

[182] Edmondson, Amanda. "Psychological Safety and Learning Behavior in Work Teams." *Administrative Science Quarterly*, vol. 44, 1 June 1999, pp. 350-83, journals.sagepub.com/doi/pdf/10.2307/2666999.

[183] Cheeks, Maura. "The Psychic Stress of Being the Only Black Woman at Work." *Lenny Letter*, 12 Jan. 2018, www.lennyletter.com/story/the-stress-of-being-the-only-black-woman-at-work.

[184] Brunschwig Graf, Martine, and Sylvie Jacquat. "Communiqué De Presse - Droits Fondamentaux: La Liberté d'Expression Trouve Sa Limite Avec Le Respect De La Dignité Humaine." *Commission Fédérale Contre le Racisme*, 30 Sept. 2019, www.ekr.admin.ch/home/f112.html. https://www.ekr.admin.ch/home/f112.html

[185] For my non-Swiss readers, you might be surprised to learn that—in very general terms—not only does termination of certain types of work contracts in Switzerland carry prescribed month-long notice periods during which an employee continues to be paid but that pregnancy (among other conditions) can freeze a notice period, essentially keeping someone on payroll for as long as a year+ in some cases. As you can surmise, one of the intentions behind this legal protection is to dissuade employers from firing women for becoming pregnant. See "Pregnancy and Motherhood: Employee Protection." Translated by Drew Lilley, SECO - Swiss Confederation, State Secretariat for Economic Affairs, Labour Directorate, 14 June 2014, www.seco.admin.ch/dokumentation/publikation.

Chapter Nine: Mentorship—The Secret Ingredient to a Great Career

[186] "Oprah Winfrey: Who Mentored Oprah Winfrey?" *Harvard School of Public Health*, 13 Jan. 2013, sites.sph.harvard.edu/wmy/celebrities/oprah-winfrey/.

[187] Mochari, Ilan. "Steve Job's Early Advice to Mark Zuckerberg: Go East." *Inc.com*, 29 Sep. 2015, www.inc.com/ilan-mochari/visit-india-creativity.html.

[188] D'Onfro, Jillian. "Mark Zuckerberg Says That Visiting an Indian Temple at the Urging of Steve Jobs Helped Him Stick to Facebook's Mission." *Business Insider*, 27 Sept. 2015, www.businessinsider.com/mark-zuckerberg-visited-india-thanks-to-steve-jobs-2015-9?r=US&IR=T.

[189] If you are like me, your eyebrows shot up when you read "we" (Americans) versus "the people in the Indian

countryside" ("them") in recognition of the racist and classist implications of that dichotomy. It is compelling, more so, for that very reason because it demonstrates both the ills and the complexity of a mentor/mentee relationship in terms of communication, identity, and empathy. Would the relationship have been the same had Zuckerberg been Brown or Black?

[190] Isaacson, Walter. "The Genius of Jobs." *The New York Times*, 29 Oct. 2011, www.nytimes.com/2011/10/30/opinion/sunday/steve-jobss-genius.html.

[191] Eugenio, Sheila. "7 Reasons You Need a Mentor for Entrepreneurial Success." *Entrepreneur*, 17 Aug. 2016, www.entrepreneur.com/article/280134.

[192] Drewis, Deena. "Why Is It So Hard for Black Women to Find Mentors?" *Girlboss*, 16 Feb. 2018, www.girlboss.com/work/2018-2-20-find-a-mentor-women-of-color.

[193] "Finding the Mentor You Need." *Latinas Uprising*, 3 Sept. 2019, latinasuprising.com/mentors-for-latina-lawyers/.

[194] Drewis, Deena. "Why Is It So Hard for Black Women to Find Mentors?" *Girlboss*, 16 Feb. 2018, www.girlboss.com/work/2018-2-20-find-a-mentor-women-of-color.

[195] While Latinos are being offered more speaking roles in television and film, it is clear that depictions of "the wide variety of the Latino experience are more the exception than the rule. And when it comes to representation of Afro-Latinos, indigenous, or LGBTQ Latinx on TV, you'd have to look long and hard to find even a couple appearances." See Betancourt, Manuel. "There Are More Latinos on TV, But Is That Really Progress?" *Remezcla*, 5 Jan. 2018, remezcla.com/features/film/latino-representation-television-2017/.

[196] Lee, Jesse. "The President's Nominee: Judge Sonia Sotomayor." National Archives and Records Administration, 26 May 2009, obamawhitehouse.archives.gov/blog/2009/05/26/presidentrsquos-nominee-judge-sonia-sotomayor.

[197] Sotomayor, Sonia. *My Beloved World*. Alfred A. Knopf, 2016.

[198] Sotomayor, Sonia. *My Beloved World*. Alfred A. Knopf, 2016, p. 178.

[199] There were few, but they were mighty. Coming from across the Americas, my Latin and Caribbean-American classmates were optimistic, hardworking, funny, talented, and smart from all night study sessions, interview hook-ups, and job advice to two a.m. paellas

after hours of dancing.

[200] Shore, Leslie. "Gal Interrupted, Why Men Interrupt Women and How to Avert This In The Workplace." *Forbes*, 3 Jan. 2017, www.forbes.com/sites/womensmedia/2017/01/03/gal-interrupted-why-men-interrupt-women-and-how-to-avert-this-in-the-workplace/#204c7f3e17c3.

[201] "Gender Study Finds 90% of People Are Biased against Women." *BBC News*, 5 Mar. 2020, www.bbc.com/news/world-51751915.

[202] Next Avenue. "When Women Are Called 'Aggressive' At Work. *Forbes*, 28 Aug. 2018, www.forbes.com/sites/nextavenue/2018/08/28/when-women-are-called-aggressive-at-work/#125a350f7bc8.

[203] Chira, Susan. "The Universal Phenomenon of Men Interrupting Women." *The New York Times*, 14 June 2017, www.nytimes.com/2017/06/14/business/women-sexism-work-huffington-kamala-harris.html.

[204] Lawler, Opheli Garcia. "Michelle Obama is Done with the Gospel of 'Lean In'." *The Cut*, 2 Dec. 2018, www.thecut.com/2018/12/michelle-obama-lean-in-becoming-book-tour.html.

[205] Obama, Michelle. *Becoming*. Crown, 2018.

[206] Weise, Elizabeth. "Sheryl Sandberg: Hard to Lean in as Single Mom." *USA Today*, Gannett Satellite Information Network, 6 May 2016, eu.usatoday.com/story/tech/news/2016/05/06/sheryl-sandberg-hard-lean-single-mom/84041588/.

[207] Larcker, David F., et al. "2013 Executive Coaching Survey." *Stanford Graduate School of Center for Leadership Development and Research*, 2013, www.gsb.stanford.edu/sites/gsb/files/publication-pdf/cgri-survey-2013-executive-coaching.pdf.

[208] Mark, Michelle. "That Iconic Photo of Obama Bending over so a Boy Could Feel His Hair Was Taken Just over 10 Years Ago. Here's the Moving Story behind It." *Insider*, 9 May 2019, www.insider.com/photo-of-boy-feeling-obamas-hair-taken-10-years-ago-2019-5.

[209] Nkomo, Morena William, et al. "Influences of Mentoring Functions on Job Satisfaction and Organizational Commitment of Graduate Employees." *Advances in Intelligent Systems and Computing Advances in Human Factors in Training, Education, and Learning Sciences*, July 2018, pp. 197-206., doi:10.1007/978-3-319-60018-5_20.

[210] Simmons, Jon. "9 Companies with Solid Mentorship Programs."

Monster Career Advice, www.monster.com/career-advice/article/9-companies-with-solid-mentorship-programs-0816.

[211] "Leadership Development: Deloitte LLP: Inclusion." *Deloitte United States*, 17 Dec. 2019, www2.deloitte.com/us/en/pages/about-deloitte/articles/inclusion-leadership-development.html.

[212] Nunez, Vivian. "5 Tips from a Latina Leadership Mentor on How to Sidestep Your Fear and Pursue Your Passions." *Forbes*, 29 July 2018, www.forbes.com/sites/viviannunez/2018/07/29/5-tips-from-a-latina-leadership-mentor-on-how-to-sidestep-your-fear-and-pursue-your-passions/#614c959d73ea.

Chapter Ten: Rev Your Entrepreneurial Engine and Take the Road

[213] Bundles, A'Lelia Perry. *Self Made: The Life and Times of Madam C. J. Walker*. John Murray, 2020, p. 88.

[214] Koji, David. "An Inspiring Discussion with Simon Sinek About Learning Your 'Why'." *Entrepreneur*, 14 Feb. 2020, www.entrepreneur.com/article/284791.

[215] Smith, Chris. "Don't Hire Entrepreneurs; Hire Entrepreneurial Spirit." *Harvard Business Review*, 7 Aug. 2014, hbr.org/2013/02/dont-hire-entrepreneurs-hire-e.

[216] Council, Young Entrepreneur. "5 Ways to Apply Entrepreneurship Principles to Any Career." *Business Insider*, 9 Aug. 2012, www.businessinsider.com/5-ways-to-apply-entrepreneurship-principles-to-any-career-2012-8?r=US&IR=T.

[217] Llopis, Glenn. "Working with an Entrepreneurial Attitude Is a Powerful Addiction." *Forbes*, 15 Jan. 2013, www.forbes.com/sites/glennllopis/2013/01/15/working-with-an-entrepreneurial-attitude-is-a-powerful-addiction/#5f146dc96320.

[218] Smith, Chris. "Don't Hire Entrepreneurs; Hire Entrepreneurial Spirit." *Harvard Business Review*, 7 Aug. 2014, hbr.org/2013/02/dont-hire-entrepreneurs-hire-e.

[219] Goleman, Daniel. *Focus: the Hidden Driver of Excellence*. Harper, 2015.

[220] Goleman, Daniel. "Daniel Goleman on Focus: The Secret to High Performance and Fulfilment." YouTube, 2 Nov. 2013, www.youtube.com/watch?v=HTfYv3IEOqM.

[221] Goleman, Daniel. "Leadership: The Focused Leader." *Harvard Business Review*, Dec. 2013, www.meltonschool.org/images/students-

leadership-pdfs/focused-leader.pdf.

[222] Jarrett, Christian. "The Neuroscience of Decision Making Explained in 30 Seconds." *Wired*, Conde Nast, 10 Mar. 2014, www.wired.com/2014/03/neuroscience-decision-making-explained-30-seconds/.

[223] Baer, Drake. "How Only Being Able to Use Logic to Make Decisions Destroyed a Man's Life." *The Cut*, 14 June 2016, www.thecut.com/2016/06/how-only-using-logic-destroyed-a-man.html.

[224] Idem.

[225] Sinek, Simon. *Start with Why: How Great Leaders Inspire Everyone to Take Action*, Portfolio, 2009.

[226] Sinek, Simon. *Leaders Eat Last Why Some Teams Pull Together and Others Don't*. Portfolio/Penguin, 2017.

[227] Sinek, Simon. "How Great Leaders Inspire Action." *TED*, Sept. 2009, www.ted.com/talks/simon_sinek_how_great_leaders_inspire_action?language=en.

[228] Idem.

[229] Idem.

[230] Horowitz, Sara. "Why Are More Women Than Men Freelancing?" *Fast Company*, 10 Mar. 2015, www.fastcompany.com/3043455/why-are-more-women-than-men-freelancing.

[231] Horowitz, Sara. "Sara Horowitz, Founder and Executive Director, Freelancers Union." YouTube, 20 Jan. 2015, www.youtube.com/watch?v=rH7KYvWq0-w.

[232] Fox, Justin. "Breaking Down the Freelance Economy." *Harvard Business Review*, 6 Dec. 2017, hbr.org/2014/09/breaking-down-the-freelance-economy.

[233] Lapowsky, Issie. "How Small Business Makes People Healthy." *Inc.com*, 3 Apr. 2012, www.inc.com/magazine/201204/issie-lapowsky/small-business-does-a-body-good.html.

[234] Rose, Greg. "Why We All Need Growth Mindsets." *Virgin*, 27 Apr. 2017, www.virgin.com/richard-branson/why-we-all-need-growth-mindsets.

Chapter Eleven: You Know It Now. I Knew It Then. It's Time to Go.

[235] Frost, Robert. "The Road Not Taken." *Poetry*

Foundation, www.poetryfoundation.org/poems/44272/the-road-not-taken, 11 Mar. 2020.

[236] Gilchrist, Karen. "When Resigning, Here's Why You Should Never Accept That Counteroffer." *CNBC*, 11 Mar. 2019, www.cnbc.com/2018/05/07/resignation-tips-why-you-should-never-accept-that-counteroffer.html.

[237] Idem.

[238] Doyle, Alison. "Top 10 Good Reasons to Quit Your Job." *The Balance Careers*, 3 Sept. 2019, www.thebalancecareers.com/top-good-reasons-to-quit-your-job-2061010.

[239] Taylor, Beth. "When Your Gut Says, 'It's Time to Quit'." *PayScale*, 5 Sept. 2014, www.payscale.com/career-news/2014/09/when-your-gut-says-its-time-to-quit.

[240] Mayer, Emeran A. "Gut Feelings: The Emerging Biology of Gut-Brain Communication." *Nature Reviews Neuroscience*, U.S. National Library of Medicine, 13 July 2011, www.ncbi.nlm.nih.gov/pubmed/21750565.

[241] Idem.

[242] "14 Effective Employee Retention Strategies." Robert Half, 6 Feb. 2020, www.roberthalf.com/blog/management-tips/effective-employee-retention-strategies.

[243] *Job Openings and Labor Turnover Survey News Release*. US Bureau of Labor Statistics, 6 Aug. 2019, www.bls.gov/news.release/archives/jolts_08062019.htm.

[244] "Mobilité Professionnelle." *Office Fédéral De La Statistique Suisse*, 17 Apr. 2020, www.bfs.admin.ch/bfs/fr/home/statistiques/travail-remuneration/activite-professionnelle-temps-travail/actifs-occupes/mobilite-professionnelle.html.

[245] "Turnover and Retention: Quick Take." *Catalyst*, 16 Apr. 2020, www.catalyst.org/research/turnover-and-retention/.

[246] "News Release." *Bureau of Labor Statistics, U.S. Department of Labor*, 15 May 2020, www.bls.gov/news.release/pdf/jolts.pdf.

[247] Bailey, Grant. "This Is How Many Days the Average British Person Will Work in Their Lifetime, Survey Says." *The Independent*, Independent Digital News and Media, 26 Sept. 2018, www.independent.co.uk/life-stylebritish-people-work-days-lifetime-overtime-quit-job-survey-study-a8556146.html.

[248] Bialik, Carl. "Seven Careers in a Lifetime? Think Twice, Researchers Say." *The Wall Street Journal*, 4 Sept. 2010, www.wsj.com/articles/SB10001424052748704206804575468162805877990.

[249] "Turnover and Retention: Quick Take." *Catalyst*, 16 Apr. 2020, www.catalyst.org/research/turnover-and-retention/.

[250] "Economic News Release: Employee Tenure Summary in 2018." *U.S. Bureau of Labor Statistics*, 20 Sept. 2018, www.bls.gov/news.release/tenure.nr0.htm.

[251] Weiner, Zoe. "9 Things to Do After You Quit Your Job." *Bustle*, 7 Oct. 2015, www.bustle.com/articles/115422-9-things-to-do-after-you-quit-your-job-from-someone-who-just-did-it.

Chapter Twelve: Deciding to Stay and Pursue Perfection

[252] "Jiro Dreams of Sushi." *IMDb*, 2011, www.imdb.com/title/tt1772925/characters/nm4807635.

[253] Gordinier, Jeff. "Make Sure the Nigiri Doesn't Miss Its Cue." *The New York Times*, 28 Feb. 2012, www.nytimes.com/2012/02/29/dining/jiro-ono-a-sushi-legend-is-captured-in-a-new-documentary.html?_r=0.

[254] "Jiro Dreams of Sushi." *IMDb*, 2011, www.imdb.com/title/tt1772925/characters/nm4807635.

[255] Emerson, Ralph Waldo. "Experience." *Essays: Second Series*, 1844, emersoncentral.com/texts/essays-second-series/experience. Accessed at 3 Aug. 2020.

[256] Gladwell, Malcolm. "Outliers: The Story of Success." Little Brown & Co., 2008, pp. 38-41.

[257] Idem, at p. 39.

[258] Juma, Aly. "Shokunin and Sushi: What Jiro Can Teach Us About Mastery." *Medium*, 6 Oct. 2017, medium.com/@alyjuma/shokunin-and-sushi-what-jiro-can-teach-us-about-mastery-1a886f129df4.

[259] Benson, Richard. "The Rise of the Handmade Hipster," *Esquire*. 27 Oct. 2015, www.esquire.com/uk/style/fashion/news/a9034/the-rise-of-the-hipster/.

[260] Kent, Beck, et al. "Manifesto for Agile Software Development." *Agilemanifesto.org*, 15 May 2020, agilemanifesto.org.

[261] "Introduction to Software Craftsmanship." *javajee.com*, 18 Feb. 2015, javajee.com/introduction-to-software-craftsmanship.

[262] Peter, Norvig. "Why Is Everyone in Such a Rush?" *Teach*

Yourself Programming in Ten Years, norvig.com/21-days.html. http://norvig.com/21-days.html.

[263] Bertog, Kelly. "My Worst Day: J.K. Rowling." *Medium*, 28 July 2019, medium.com/@kellybertog/my-worst-day-j-k-rowling-f99bc7c33168.

[264] Reed, Jay. "J.K. Rowling, Who Denies Being a Billionaire, Made $54 Million Last Year. Here's How the Famous 'Harry Potter' Author Makes and Spends Her Fortune." *Business Insider*, 16 Apr. 2019, www.businessinsider.com/jk-rowling-harry-potter-net-worth-author-millions-fortune-lifestyle-2019-4?r=US&IR=T.

[265] Duffy, James. "Malcolm Gladwell's 10000 Hours Rule Explained." *More Than Accountants*, 23 July 2020, www.morethanaccountants.co.uk/malcolm-gladwells-10000-hours-rule-explained/.

[266] Irish, Emily. "The Craftsman Approach: Master Your Work Through Deliberate Practice." *Zapier*, 12 May 2020, zapier.com/blog/master-your-work/.

[267] Goleman, Daniel. "Daniel Goleman on Focus: The Secret to High Performance and Fulfilment." YouTube, 2 Nov. 2013, www.youtube.com/watch?v=HTfYv3IEOqM.

[268] Mindful Staff. "Jon Kabat-Zinn: Defining Mindfulness." *Mindful*, 11 Jan. 2019, www.mindful.org/jon-kabat-zinn-defining-mindfulness/.

[269] Gelles, David. "How to Be More Mindful at Work." *The New York Times*, Sept. 2019, www.nytimes.com/guides/well/be-more-mindful-at-work.

[270] Idem.

[271] LearnVest. "Your 'High-Earning Years': Salary Secrets for Your 20s, 30s and 40s." *Forbes*, 13 Jan. 2014, www.forbes.com/sites/learnvest/2014/01/13/your-high-earning-years-salary-secrets-for-your-20s-30s-and-40s/#273a00b2201e.

Chapter Thirteen: We Want You! Stand Up and Lead.

[272] Washington Post Staff. "Transcript: Read Michelle Obama's Full Speech from the 2016 DNC." *The Washington Post*, WP Company, 26 July 2016, www.washingtonpost.com/news/post-politics/wp/2016/07/26/transcript-read-michelle-obamas-full-speech-from-the-2016-dnc/.

[273] Bruner, Raisa. "Michelle Obama Explains What 'Going High' Really

Means." *Time*, 20 Nov. 2018, time.com/5459984/michelle-obama-go-high/.

[274] Warren, Katie. "Forbes Just Revoked Kylie Jenne's Billionaire Status, Saying She's Exaggerated Her Compan's Success for Years. Take a Look at How Jenner Built Her Empire." *Business Insider*, 29 May 2020, www.businessinsider.com/how-does-kylie-jenner-make-money-2018-7?r=US&IR=T#but-a-new-investigation-by-forbes-has-called-jenners-billionaire-status-into-question-2.

[275] "Jay Shetty 30 Under 30—2017." *Forbes*, 7 June 2020, www.forbes.com/profile/jay-shetty/#29a000084f66.

[276] Berg, Madeline. "The Highest-Paid YouTube Stars of 2019: The Kids Are Killing It." *Forbes*, 18 Dec. 2019, www.forbes.com/sites/maddieberg/2019/12/18/the-highest-paid-youtube-stars-of-2019-the-kids-are-killing-it/#b36e91438cd4.

[277] Sinek, Simon. "How Great Leaders Inspire Action." *TED*, Sept. 2009, www.ted.com/talks/simon_sinek_how_great_leaders_inspire_action?language=en.

[278] Sinek, Simon. "Leaders Eat Last Why Some Teams Pull Together and Others Don't." Portfolio/Penguin, 2017.

[279] Brown Brené. *Daring Greatly: How the Courage to Be Vulnerable Transforms the Way We Live, Love, Parent, and Lead*. Avery, an Imprint of Penguin Random House, 2015.

[280] Brown, Brené. *Dare to Lead: Brave Work, Tough Conversations, Whole Hearts*. Random House Large Print Publishing, 2019.

[281] "'Dare to Lead': Brené Brown Says Vulnerability Is the 'Only Path to Courage.'" YouTube, CBS This Morning, 10 Oct. 2018, www.youtube.com/watch?v=hEnqV_M_Dm4.

[282] Knight, Rebecca. "How to Make Your One-on-Ones with Employees More Productive." *Harvard Business Review*, 21 Nov. 2016, hbr.org/2016/08/how-to-make-your-one-on-ones-with-employees-more-productive. https://hbr.org/2016/08/how-to-make-your-one-on-ones-with-employees-more-productive

[283] Fournier, Camille. "Keynote: Building and Motivating Engineering Teams." Open Source Leadership Summit 2017, www.camilletalk.com.

[284] Shinagel, Michael. "The Paradox of Leadership." *Harvard Division of Continuing Learning*, Harvard University, 3 July 2013, www.extension.harvard.edu/professional-development/blog/paradox-leadership.

[285] Lizza, Ryan. "Leading from Behind." *The New Yorker,* 19 June 2017, www.newyorker.com/news/news-desk/leading-from-behind.

[286] Idem.

[287] Sinek, Simon. *Leaders Eat Last Why Some Teams Pull Together and Others Don't.* Portfolio/Penguin, 2017.

[288] Idem.

[289] Abadi, Mark. "When CEO Satya Nadella Took over Microsoft, He Started Defusing Its Toxic Culture by Handing Each of His Execs a 15-Year-Old Book by a Psychologist." *Business Insider,* 7 Oct. 2018, www.businessinsider.com/microsoft-satya-nadella-nonviolent-communication-2018-10?r=US&IR=T.

[290] Stahl, Ashley. "Just Promoted to Manager? Here Are 5 Strategies for Success." *Forbes,* 7 Aug. 2015, www.forbes.com/sites/ashleystahl/2015/04/16/just-promoted-to-manager-here-are-5-strategies-for-success/#76e37f007c58.

[291] Pretty Young Professional. "7 Tips to Succeed as a First-Time Manager." *Business Insider,* 22 May 2011, www.businessinsider.com/7-to-dos-as-a-first-time-manager-2011-5?r=US&IR=T.

[292] Stahl, Ashley. "Just Promoted to Manager? Here Are 5 Strategies for Success." *Forbes,* 7 Aug. 2015, www.forbes.com/sites/ashleystahl/2015/04/16/just-promoted-to-manager-here-are-5-strategies-for-success/#76e37f007c58.

[293] McCarthy, Dan. "Challenges Managers Face (and How to Deal with Them)." *The Balance Careers,* 19 Nov. 2019, www.thebalancecareers.com/top-challenges-a-manager-will-face-2275955, and Officevibe Content Team, "Overcoming 12 Challenges That First-Time Managers Face." *Officevibe,* 13 May 2020, www.officevibe.com/blog/challenges-first-time-managers.

[294] Agyei, Steve. "A Man is but the Product of His Thoughts What He Thinks, He Becomes." *Medium,* 22 Dec. 2016, medium.com/@steveagyei65/a-man-is-but-the-product-of-his-thoughts-what-he-thinks-he-becomes-36881cafbd2b.

[295] Munzenrieder, Kyle. "The Gospel According to RuPaul: 10 Inspiring Quotes Before the Return of RuPaul's Drag Race." *W Magazine,* 19 Mar. 2017, www.wmagazine.com/story/rupaul-inspiring-quotes-rupauls-drag-race.

Chapter Fourteen: When Everything Else Has Failed…

[296] Thomson, J. A. K. *The Ethics of Aristotle: the Nichomachean Ethics.* Penguin, 1976, p. 43.

[297] Steindl-Rast, David. "Want to be happy? Be grateful." *TEDGlobal 2013*, June 2013, www.ted.com/talks/david_steindl_rast_want_to_be_happy_be_grateful.

[298] Inman, Matthew. "How to Be Perfectly Unhappy." *The Oatmeal*, 15 May 2019, theoatmeal.com/comics/unhappy.

[299] Idem.

[300] Oswald, Andrew J., et al. "Happiness and Productivity." *Econstor*, Leibniz Information Centre for Economics, Dec. 2009, www.econstor.eu/bitstream/10419/35451/1/522164196.pdf.

[301] Rampton, John. "Want a Happier Work Atmosphere? Science Says to Follow These 10 Tips." *Inc.com*, 29 Aug. 2017, www.inc.com/john-rampton/what-makes-people-happy-when-they-work.html.

[302] Brown Brené. *Braving the Wilderness: the Quest for True Belonging and the Courage to Stand Alone.* Random House, 2019, p. 78.

[303] Krapivin, Pavel. "How Google's Strategy for Happy Employees Boosts Its Bottom Line." *Forbes*, 27 Sept. 2018, www.forbes.com/sites/pavelkrapivin/2018/09/17/how-googles-strategy-for-happy-employees-boosts-its-bottom-line/#25b1fac22fc4.

[304] Fauver, Larry, et al. "Does It Pay to Treat Employees Well? International Evidence on the Value of Employee-Friendly Culture." *Journal of Corporate Finance*, North-Holland, 24 Feb. 2018, www.sciencedirect.com/science/article/pii/S092911991730740X.

[305] Idem.

[306] DePamphilis, Donald M. "Mergers, Acquisitions, and Other Restructuring Activities: an Integrated Approach to Process, Tools, Cases, and Solutions." 10th ed., Academic Press, an Imprint of Elsevier, 2019, pp. 65–98.

[307] Su, Amy Jen, and Muriel Maignan Wilkins. "What Gets in the Way of Listening." *Harvard Business Review*, 14 Apr. 2014, hbr.org/2014/04/what-gets-in-the-way-of-listening.

[308] Angelou, Maya. "Dr. Maya Angelou's 3-Word Secret to Living Your Best Life." *Oprah's Master Class*, OWN, 28 May 2014, www.youtube.com/watch?v=sr6LMr-rXEc.

[309] Allende, Isabel. "Isabel Allende: How to Live Passionately—No Matter Your Age." YouTube, TED, 3 Sept. 2014, www.youtube.com/

watch?v=5ifMRNag2XU.

ACKNOWLEDGEMENT

I wish to thank all my interviewees. You gifted me your stories, fears, and hopes with a vulnerability and authenticity that far exceeds my attempt to capture and distill them. This year that I spent with you changed my life—I hope it is a gift I can share. I wish to thank in particular Didi and Ilaria. Your intelligence, work ethic, and professionalism are equally inspired as they are inspiring. Many of the better ideas in this book came from our conversations. I hope that my words are worthy of your investment and your friendship. Thank you as well to my editors and first readers. Your encouragement was my flashlight in the dark.

Muchas gracias a mi familia, en particular mi Mami que siempre me ha dado lo mejor que podía. Bien te nombraron Socorro, Mami, porque siempre has estado para ayudarme en un mundo grande y extraño. Daddy, you left us far too early; I hope I have fulfilled your dreams. Gracias a Helen, Rodry y Pablo A., ustedes son mis alma-hermanos, que me han aguantado y querido desde que fui una gordita rebelde, es decir, siempre. Helen, hermanita chiquita y bajita, you are mi inspiration, a warrior, an artist, and a leader. Your belief in me became part of my spinal cord. Thank you. À Marie-Louise, ma deuxième maman, merci pour ton amour, tes mots sages et ta compréhension. Tu m'inspire avec ton esprit ouvert, passionnée et authentique. Thank you also to my nieces and nephew who bring us constant wonder and joy. Mis queridos Pablo, Carmen y Teo, thank you for the time you gave me for this project, for your constant faith, love, and support, and for your wise counsel. I believe in you. I love you. You are my Everything. Thank you, thank you, thank you.

And to you, my Dear Reader, for the privilege of your time and your thoughts, I will be forever grateful and humbled by your choice to spend a bit of time here. I pray I have done right by you and that the off-the-clock moments we have shared have enriched your life as the telling has enriched mine.

ABOUT THE AUTHOR

C. P. M.

C. P. MacMaster is a Colombian-American expat residing in Geneva, Switzerland alongside cherished family, friends, and colleagues. She fervently believes in the incorrigible alchemy of a good campfire, a gripping story, and savage optimism to light even the most starless night.

www.ingramcontent.com/pod-product-compliance
Lightning Source LLC
Chambersburg PA
CBHW071449220526
45472CB00003B/739